Pivot to Product Manager

Pivot to Product Manager

The ultimate 3-Step playbook to kick start your Product Management career

Irving Malcolm

Just for You

A FREE GIFT TO OUR READERS

Check out our guide on overcoming the key frustrations that every New Product Manager will face. Learn the keys to converting those challenges into a launching pad for your success! Visit this link:

https://www.irvingmalcolm.com/resources/

Contents

Introduction

> "Learn as though you would never be able to master it; hold it as though you would be in fear of losing it."
>
> – Confucius, Chinese Philosopher and Teacher

Technology has been one of the fastest-growing industries for the past few decades, and we still expect to see exponential growth in this industry. We are dependent on many technology-based products in our daily lives, be it our communication apps or our health trackers. We know that an excellent product is usually a result of a robust Product Manager's vision, skill, and leadership.

This book is here to help you move into a Product Manager role and build products that customers will love and rely on. This book is for everyone who is either curious about this role or has recently decided to pivot to this thriving career path. You may be a techie, a business buff, or someone with an eye for good user experience; this role welcomes all who are curious enough to learn new things and enjoy building and launching products that matter to their users.

This published work has been a labor of love for me, as I also made this pivot years ago, and I understand all the ups and downs of this exciting journey. But trust me when I tell you that learning is the only way forward, and as a future Product Manager, you will be jumping into new tasks daily. I don't promise it will be an easy journey, but this book will provide you with the right knowledge and tools you need to get there.

The Product Manager's role is not a new one and was previously reserved only for professionals building physical products. Yet, with the onset of the software revolution, we have watched this role seep into most tech-focused organizations. Currently, it is one of the highest-paid roles in the technology industry, and the demand for talented Product Managers isn't going away anytime soon.

Your job as the product manager will be to lead most of the design, business, and technical decision-making around a product. The Product Manager may or may not have a direct team reporting to them, but they are the ones calling most of the shots for the Product itself. This role lies at the intersection of design, technology, and business, but you don't have to be an expert on all of them. The primary function is to work closely with the team of experts, researching, learning, and making better-informed decisions with the help of all the people involved in the product development process. This role is scientific and data-driven but simultaneously requires creative intuition and the ability to trust your instincts.

You will not only work closely with the product teams but be the voice of your current or prospective users. You will be their advocate on the product team, and your goal is to make them fall in love with your Product.

You will also need to be the chief evangelist of your Product, and your work is not only to build something but to ensure it reaches as many people as possible.

So, let's get into the actual contents of this book and how it can help you land a job as a Product Manager.

The book is divided into three sections, with a few bonus chapters at the end. It is written in a way that is easy to read and follow through by a busy professional. Throughout the book, you will find many examples and practice questions to improve your understanding of the different concepts and skillsets required to land this role. This three-step process will take you closer to your dream role as a 'PM'.

Section one covers what you should know and be prepared for before pivoting to the Product Manager role. This will include some basic concepts related to the field, the difference between a few similar-sounding roles, different paths towards the Product Management role, the importance and need for certifications, and making the best use of side projects.

Section two contains helpful information and questions for you to prepare for the interview. This section only has one chapter but is essential to read before you start requesting interviews with a potential employer. We will talk about choosing the right company for you by thorough research, learning about the type of PM roles they already have or may prefer to hire, preparing for onsite vs. remote interviews, and some generally helpful interviewing tips and techniques.

The third section is all about the Product Management interview process, and each chapter covers a specific concept or function related to the job. It starts with writing, rehearsing, and delivering your elevator pitch and then moving onto more specific topics related to Product Management.

You will learn how to decode and answer questions related to:

- Product strategy
- Estimation techniques
- Technical feasibility and implementation
- Key Performance Indicators ('KPIs') and metrics
- Product business models, and
- Pricing strategies

All of these are fundamental aspects of this job, and you must demonstrate understanding and some competency in them to pass the interview process. This section has examples and practice questions for you to work on and prepare, so don't worry, we've got you covered.

The last chapter of section three covers the behavioral traits of a Product Manager. These may appear deceivingly simple, but it is the hardest part of an interview, as every hiring manager is looking for someone with a specific set of personality traits. The person who will get hired will be an excellent personality-company fit and someone who is innovative and authentic.

There are two bonus chapters at the end of the book and a glossary of Product Management terms. The first bonus chapter is about the PM mindset. It includes the four mindsets and how you can build each of them to do a better job as a Product Manager. You will also be learning about cognitive biases and core Product

Management skills, including user advocacy, product evangelism, strategic and analytical thinking, and the ability to lead and communicate.

The second bonus chapter is about Software Development practices and will give you insights into building technology products. Having this knowledge can help you in the interview process and during your career as a Product Manager.

This section also includes a glossary with the most used Product Management terms. I would recommend going through these 100 terms, as they are usually mentioned in the Product Management interviews, and knowing them well can be a massive plus for you.

I wrote this book, and you are reading it because we both know that a good resume or reference will only get you one foot in the door. The actual evaluation happens during the interview, and most of the companies do multiple interviews to gauge a candidate's aptitude. The hiring decision-making process can be pretty complex, depending on the organization.

These interviews usually require you to comprehend the situation or the question presented to you and verbalize your thinking process in front of the interviewer. Not all interviews, or interviewers, are the same; but they all look for similar skill sets and attitudes in a Product Manager.

So here, I am leaving you with a few tips to make this learning process simpler for you.

- All the best PMs I have met are interested in reading, either for pleasure or for work. Make it your habit to read for at least 30 minutes a day.

You will find a list of 50 recommended books at the very end. I have read them all, and some of them I have read multiple times.

- Create a time and money budget for this pivot. Pencil in the learning time in your weekly schedule and set aside a reasonable budget for learning materials and activities, as well as for joining any paid networks or communities.

- Subscribe to multiple technology and business-related online publications, like Mashable, TechCrunch, HackerNews, and VentureBeat. You will not only pick up the current happenings in the ecosystem but will also find excellent experience and advice-sharing articles related to product management, technology, and the entrepreneurial space.

- While you are reading this book, keep a notebook or your note-taking device handy. Annotate the text, take notes, reread the examples, practice the questions and work on the given action items at the end of each chapter. This will help you in preparing for the product management interview better than just reading through the book alone. Remember, only practice will make you perfect.

- Find your tribe, and this can be a community of Product Managers on social media or a mentor network, be it free or paid. Talking to people who are already doing the work is imperative. It will help you learn, but they can also refer you for learning and work opportunities and give you practical advice and guidance.

It took a lot of hard work and perseverance, not only from me but also from a whole group of people, including my team and the people engaged in the publishing side. I am beyond grateful that I could complete this important and enormous project and, for you as you have chosen to spend your money and time on this book.

Thank you, and happy learning!

Irving Malcolm

SECTION-I
BEFORE YOU PIVOT

STEP 1: Get to know the role and some possible paths leading towards it.

1

INSIDE THIS CHAPTER

- ☑ **Product Management**

- ☑ **Functions of Product Management**

- ☑ **Role of a Product Manager**

- ☑ **Product Development Life Cycle**

- ☑ **Product Roadmaps**

- ☑ **A Day in the Life of a Product Manager**

- ☑ **Decoding the Three PMs**

- ☑ **Action Items**

- ☑ **Chapter Takeaways**

What You Should Know Before You Pivot

"

A great product manager has the brain of an engineer, the heart of a designer, and the speech of a diplomat.

– Deep Nishar, Vice President of Product at LinkedIn

Making the right career move can be very rewarding, both in terms of money and job satisfaction. In today's world, where access to information is cheap and abundantly available, learning a new skill set or upgrading your existing craft is easier than ever before. Exploring this idea to pivot into a Product Management role can be an excellent exercise in creating your skill inventory, as well as in self-reflection.

This first chapter is all about understanding Product Management, the role of a Product Manager, and some key concepts and terms related to this career path. We want to start with the basics, and our goal here is to get you excited for this career move.

Product Management

First things first, let's talk about what Product Management is.

Simply put, Product Management is the process that leads the planning, development, launch, growth, and maintenance of a Product and is pivotal in the success or failure of the Product.

Though the process itself is relatively consistent across the industry, the responsibilities of the Product Manager role vary from company to company. At the core of it, the function is an interaction between design, technology, and business. Still, the responsibilities are different, depending upon the type, size, and stage of the Product and the culture of the company. Some companies prefer technical Product Managers, and others will prefer someone from a business or growth background. Some will look for Product Managers who are subject matter experts (or SME's). We will do a deep dive on this topic in Chapter 3.

Functions of Product Management

These three functions, design, technology, and business, are imperative for a product's launch and success. A product manager doesn't have to be an expert in all these functions, but having a solid grip is critical to working effectively with these areas and make better decisions. Let's have a closer look at them:

- Technology or engineering: When we say technology or engineering, we mean the teams building the software and hardware components of the Product. Without technology, the idea will stay an idea.

- Design: This means everything that impacts the interaction between the Product and the user. It is about the ease of use and aesthetics of the Product, including both user interface and user experience.

- Business: This means two specific things; value for the user that converts into revenue for the company and the teams that work on money-related questions, including pricing, marketing, sales, and forecasting.

Role of a Product Manager

The Product Manager is a strategic role, and most Product Managers don't get involved in managing the team's day-to-day activities. Their focus stays on realizing the Product's vision, as opposed to daily task allocations and status reports.

A Product Manager works with several stakeholders to ensure that the Product's strategic objectives are realized, and they actively contribute to building a product their customers will love to use.

One of the great things about this role is that it welcomes various educational backgrounds and experiences. I have seen Product Managers from a wide range of distinct fields, from the liberal arts, or engineering, through to medicine or finance. Because of their varied backgrounds, Product Managers' skillsets and ideas are more valuable to their teams. The skills required for being a Product Manager are transferable, in so much as anyone can learn and practice them. Also, because they are principally soft skills, they don't require you to have technical degrees or hands-on coding experience.

Researching, learning, strategizing, prioritizing, communicating, and executing items from their product roadmap is what a Product Manager will spend most of their time doing. This work ensures everyone is aligned with the end goal. They are usually talking to a product team's design, technology, and business functions while communicating with investors, executives, and users to ensure transparency and consistent buy-in. Central to these activities are two key elements:

i. The Product Development Life Cycle, and

ii. The Product Roadmap.

We will look at these concepts briefly in the following section.

Product Development Life Cycle

A product development life cycle has four broad phases that contain the start to a product's end. Product Managers stay active throughout the Product's life cycle, aiming to solve a different set of problems for each phase.

- **Launch:** It starts with the Launch of a product. This is where a Product Manager puts the Product in front of their users. In this phase, the focus is on collecting early user feedback and seeing if the Product does what it intends to in real-world scenarios.

- **Growth:** This is where you see the Product picking up more traction. The Product Manager must now work on different challenges, such as maintaining the Product's performance, fixing problems, and implementing new features.

- **Maturity:** Here, the number of new users starts to decrease, but the Product Manager may see new competition or disruptors coming to snatch the market share. By this phase, the Product has grown, both in size and complexity.

- **Decline:** This is where a Product Manager will see users quitting the Product, possibly due to several reasons. In some cases, the market needs have changed. In others, leaner and more innovative products are now catering to your users. At this stage, most Product Managers will pivot to a new problem to solve.

Every successful Product that you see goes through the same process. Take a moment and think about all the products you've discovered and loved using. Note my use of the past tense; you will be able to grasp how each Product went through the same life cycle, but then it was either replaced with a more advanced product or the need for that Product changed entirely. (Levitt, T. 1965.)

Product Roadmaps

At the core of a Product Manager's work is a living artifact called a Product Roadmap. This is a document of the evolution of the Product they have inside their head. The roadmap is shared amongst all three functions of the team and is used as a strategic guide for planning new features or deciding on a course of action for the Product.

This is different from a feature list or a plan, as it doesn't get into the minutiae of execution but instead stays focused on a high-level vision, strategy, and goals. A good roadmap has the following components:

- **Product Vision:** This is where a Product Manager wants the Product to be in the near future.
- **Product Strategy:** This is a high-level plan of action to reach the product vision.
- **Objectives:** Time-bound and measurable goals of your Product.
- **Initiatives:** Themes that group product features together.
- **Features:** These are the areas of functionality that you need to build to achieve your product objectives and add value to your future consumer
- **Timeframe:** All features need a date for completion.
- **Progress Markers:** These are used to measure advances on feature development.
- **Metrics:** They are used to measure progress on objectives. *(Product Roadmap: Key Features, Types, Building Tips, and Roadmap Examples, 2020)*

This action plan is not static; it will change as you get new information and find reasons to reprioritize your future activities. It is also not a linear guide, wherein the implementation details can change where necessary, at the product team's discretion.

There are plenty of tools out there that can help you with creating a product roadmap. But you don't need a specialized fancy piece of software to build a roadmap; a pen and paper will do to start sketching out this plan of action for your Product.

A Day in the Life of a Product Manager

A Product Manager role is the best profession for people who have the following attributes:

- They enjoy problem-solving.
- They are relentlessly curious.
- They thrive on the uncertainty of building and maintaining a product.

This role also requires someone who listens well and makes well-informed decisions. It is ideal for those that verbalize their thoughts, opinions and learning while staying grounded. It values evidence over opinion, but at the same time, requires people who can think outside the box. These people enjoy test running ideas to find strategies that work for the Product's business objectives.

During a typical workday for a Product Manager, they will be doing a combination of the below:

- Meeting with the different cross-functional departments of the product team; involves providing guidance while displaying a cohesive vision that ensures everyone is working to the same goals.
- Conducting user, market, and competitive research; so that they can then build upon their roadmap with new findings.
- Executing their roadmap; to achieve strategic objectives and deciding the next course of action for the Product.
- Building, prioritizing, and communicating plans; involves all stakeholders across the organization

to ensure alignment.

- Collecting user feedback and working with data; to ensure that the upcoming releases meet the Product's strategic objectives.

The role of a Product Manager isn't entirely new, and demand is consistently on the rise. By simply running a search on different job boards and professional networks, you will see hundreds of open positions available just in the big five tech companies alone (Amazon, Apple, Facebook, Google, and Microsoft). They tend to hire a lot of Product Managers. Many companies in other industries are now following suit, and you are very likely to find one that matches your skillset and career goals. There will be more on this topic in chapter 3.

The added bonus is that Product Managers are paid well, far above most countries' median salary. However, as you would imagine, not all Product Managers' earnings will be the same. A quick Google search will show you the pay scale of this role at different experience levels. An excellent website for this research is Glassdoor. The growth rate of this role is in double digits and is constantly increasing.

In summary, a Product Manager plays a leading role in an organization, as they create a vision and define the success of their Product. This role requires people who think long-term and work well with a variety of people. A PM's workdays are filled with learning and collaborative work to meet product objectives and acquire more users, resulting in more revenue for the company and value to the end customer.

Decoding the Three PMs

Before we look at preparing for the Product Manager interview process, it's essential to make a few distinctions amongst the three "PMs" functions. That is the difference between a Product Manager, Project Manager, and Program Manager. These roles sound similar and have some related responsibilities. However, they all have very different objectives and require different skills.

Project Manager

This role is tactical, and the Project Manager manages the day-to-day activities of their teams. They are responsible for work allocations, project deliverables, milestones, and budget management. The role requires technical, strategic, and leadership skills to rally a team to deliver a piece of work. They will lead an agreed-upon scope within a defined time and budget.

Program Manager

This person is responsible for multiple related projects that are collectively called a program. As opposed to a Project Manager, a Program Manager will have reporting authority. They will set high-level goals, timelines, and budgets for different projects. This is a strategic role and requires critical thinking, business acumen, and leadership skills. It is viewed as the next logical upward transition for a Senior Project Manager. Program Managers are sometimes called Super Project Managers.

Product Manager

This is the person responsible for the success of a

product and works at the strategic level. Product Managers usually work with multiple Project Managers to get different projects completed to support the success of their Product. The role requires a more nuanced approach towards market knowledge, communication, and user advocacy.

As mentioned earlier, all these roles will have varying sets of responsibilities, depending on the company's culture and business processes. When applying for any one of these roles, pay attention to the required skills, roles, and responsibilities mentioned. You will also find some certifications, or academic credentials, required for each position. We will talk about these further in chapter 2.

Action Items

For now, we are leaving you with some practical exercises to help you on this journey to pivot into the Product Manager role:

- Run an online search looking for available Product Manager roles and pay close attention to the job descriptions. See which skills or qualifications you already have. Also, match your experience with the mentioned roles and responsibilities.

- Run another search and see the best hiring companies for this role. See if you can find some salary comparisons as well. Make a list of the best-paying companies.

- Run a third search, looking at the job roles for Project, Program, and Product Managers. Observe the similarities and differences. Build an inventory of your own skills and experiences in the light of these observations.

- Find some Product Management related channels on YouTube and watch a few day-in-the-life videos of Product Managers at the big tech companies. See if their activities overlap, identify the similarities and differences.

Chapter Takeaways

To summarize, below are the takeaways from this chapter.

- A Product Management role is for a dynamic person who enjoys challenging work and can thrive on uncertainty and chaos.

- The role varies significantly from company to company and may require a slightly different skill set, but most of the skills necessary for a good Product Manager are human-centric.

- A typical workday in a Product Manager's life is full of communication, collaboration, and decision-making.

- A Project Manager, a Program Manager, and a Product Manager are three distinct roles, and they do overlap; but they require different skills and experiences.

2

INSIDE THIS CHAPTER

Pivoting to Product Management

> " Know your value add. I've seen three main PM archetypes: engineer turned PM, a designer turned PM, and businessperson turned PM. As a member of the latter bucket, I recognize that I could never out-engineer an engineer or out-design a designer. Instead, I leverage my knowledge of our business and customers to better prioritize what features make it onto the roadmap and help my team understand why we're building those features.

– Lauren Chan Lee, Director of Product Management at Care.com

As discussed in chapter 1, Product Managers come from different backgrounds and have different sets of experiences. These unique profiles make them valuable additions to product teams, as they bring irreplaceable perspectives and insights with them.

In this chapter, we will be discussing:

- The paths towards a career in Product Management

- Some tips on speeding up your career pivot
- Available levels of this exciting role
- Building side projects

Paths Towards the PM Role

There are multiple ways to get into the Product Manager role. Each of these paths will require you to be committed to learning and experimentation. In most cases, you are likely to be an experienced professional or a fresh graduate. Let's discuss both circumstances.

Finding a PM Role as an Experienced Professional

Moving to a PM role from another profession will require some level of strategic planning on your part. You may be working as a marketer or salesperson or even as an accountant. No matter what you do and where you are in your career right now, making a pivot is possible, and one of the following two scenarios may apply to you.

Scenario 1: Your Company Has a PM Division

If your current company has a Product Management division, start showing interest in their work by creating ways to make an internal move from one team or division, to another. This is a practice followed by most companies.

Don't be afraid to ask for your manager's guidance in this pivot, but don't give an ultimatum. Some managers may be willing to help you map out a development progression plan. In most cases, your manager will ask you to build a roadmap for yourself and set a timeline for making this move. This may include a course, on-the-job learning, or gaining some experience in your own time. This roadmap could be six months to a year, depending on your own learning curve and business need. Some companies may help to accelerate this process by assigning a mentor to you to prepare you for the internal move.

Scenario 2: Your Company Doesn't Have a PM Division

Getting directly into a Product Management role at a new company could be a considerable leap when you are starting out; so, the easier option would be to make a move to a similar role to yours and then make an internal pivot, as explained above.

A few roles may have a more straightforward path towards a future role in Product Management. These roles would be either customer-focused, tech-focused, or business-focused. This is because the intrinsic bank of skills is very similar to that of a Product Manager, for example:

- If you have a role in marketing or business strategy, you are already well versed in product evangelism and understand the fundamentals of business strategy.

- If you're an engineer, you already have the required technical skills and may also have expertise in a specific domain. Your domain or industry could be health, tech, fintech, logistics, etc.

- Working in Operations as a project manager, you already know how to run a team and get them to deliver valuable work items, periodically.

- A role in customer service involves learning from,

and interacting directly with, the users. Customer service people are good at communicating and understanding customer needs, wants, and frustrations.

Having the above skills and experiences will make the path a bit easier; but you still need to learn new skills specific to a Product Management role. These could include design and user experience ('UX'), analytical and strategic thinking, prioritization, and presentation skills, etc. Build your skill inventory and see what else needs to be added to it.

Finding a PM Role as a Recent Graduate

If you are a recent graduate and want to get into a Product Management career, a great entry point would be landing an Associate Product Manager program. Many tech companies offer these programs, especially in Silicon Valley. These opportunities allow the tech companies to induct graduates to be trained and mentored on Product Management. The programs are highly effective, providing mentorship, on-job training, and ample networking opportunities that allow young professionals to excel.

Some of these programs are well structured, like Google's APM program, whereas others deliberately won't be as structured. Before getting into an APM program, put your researching cap on, look at the details, and consider whether it is right for you. If you cannot find one that is available, you should start applying for entry-level jobs in companies with Product Managers. Any company with business, technology, operations, or design divisions would be an appropriate target. Then follow the advice above to make an internal move.

Tips on Speeding up Your Career Pivot

Below are a few other things that you should consider doing. These can prove advantageous for this pivot:

- **Network with the right people:** This can be done by connecting with specialized communities online, whether a Facebook group or a Slack channel. You can join a platform that works for you by participating in discussions and activities around Product Management. You can also join in-person events happening near you on Product Management, like specialized conferences and meetups.

- **Find yourself a mentor:** This can be done by following the advice above. Network with the right people and then request a mentor relationship. People are usually helpful, but you must be sure that the relationship shares mutual respect and learning, and you are always mindful of your mentor's time.

- **Participate in a hackathon:** This can be an excellent opportunity to network, find mentors, work with a team, and you can dip your toes in the world of Product Management. You will be working with a group of diverse individuals, solving a problem with a strict deadline. Hackathons are helpful in teaching both technical and interpersonal skills, and even if you don't make it to the top teams, the experience itself is worth the time and effort.

- **Informal learning:** This can be done by watching relevant video content online or reading blogs and articles related to Product Management. I would also recommend you read a few books every year on the topic to keep up with the changing landscape of the tech world. You will find a long list of recommended books and blogs at the end.

- **Get yourself certified:** Now, this can help you learn about the craft itself and show your seriousness for the pivot. It also adds credibility to your resume and will likely get you invited for an interview. I recommend that you check out Coursera and edX for their Product Management programs and nano degrees. Also, check Product School; they have a certification track and create a lot of learning content for aspiring and senior Product Managers.

- **Develop a complementing skillset:** You can learn how to code, or build prototypes and wireframes, or even learn data analytics tools. Find something that interests you, and spend time learning and practicing it. You can use both informal and formal learning approaches to reach your learning objectives.

- **Start a public learning log:** This can be a blog or a YouTube channel with content created around your learning journey. Document the process, not only for the hiring managers to see your commitment but also for other aspiring PMs. You will form a community of your own around this content and eventually can get recognized for it.

- **Build a side project:** This usually means building an app to solve a minor problem and learning all the skills required to build, launch, and maintain a small app. This can be a valuable way of learning all the subtleties of Product Management. We will touch on this later in this chapter to discuss some example projects and how you can make them work for you in an interview.

Levels of Product Management Roles

Like most other careers, Product Management roles have different levels based on experience and skill set. Here's what it looks like in most Product Development focused organizations.

- An entry-level job in Product Management is usually an **Associate Product Manager.** This role exists in large companies with an active APM program and smaller yet highly agile, product-based businesses. This is more of a tactical role focusing on defining features and working on user experience and data analytics.

- A **Product Manager** is a mid-level role, with their sole focus on product strategy and building roadmaps. They usually have a few years of experience as a Product Manager and may well have some other job experiences.

- A **Senior Product Manager** is usually managing other PMs. They will also be responsible for multiple Products within an organization.

- An executive-level role is the **VP of Product Management.** This role aligns the organizational goals with the product goals and ensures leadership buy-in in all product-related decisions.

- The topmost role in Product is **Chief Product Officer**; they oversee all Product-related activities and teams and are responsible for the success of everything that gets delivered to a user.

As an aspiring Product Manager, you will also need to work on your leadership skills. This will include the ability to:

- Communicate a vision.
- Rally your product team to achieve the strategic objectives.
- Listen and communicate with all different kinds of stakeholders
- Be the product evangelist and user advocate.
- Provide consistency and resourcefulness to your teams and stakeholders, and;
- Display empathy and self-reflection.

All these traits are essential to being a good leader, and learning them is not an overnight process. You will build your leadership muscle by continuous learning and training.

Side Projects - Should You Build One?

Now moving onto the debate around building side projects. This is a polarizing topic within the Product Management community. Some Product Managers will swear by its effectiveness, and others will tell you to do something more useful with your time. Let's expand on the arguments given by both sides to determine which one speaks more to you.

The arguments **for building** a side project are as follows:

- You work on something from scratch, showing your ability to take the initiative by learning new skills and bringing your vision to life. Nobody expects you to hire a team and work on a product that will make it "rain money". All they want to see is your commitment and your thought-process behind this side project.
- The side project doesn't necessarily have to be an

app that you have programmed yourself; instead, work on a set of wireframes, an interactive prototype, or even a business case for building a product that can solve current real-world problems. This is not only something that you can talk about in an interview but also a skill-building activity that will be considered bonus points.

Now, **the case against** side projects.

- A side project requires extra 'free time' to build. Realistically, most people have full-time employment, community, family, or care-work responsibilities. It would create an unfair advantage against people who can't commit to the extra time, even though their ideas and projects are worthwhile.

- Discussing a side project isn't always worthwhile in an interview as not all hiring managers will like what you've built. Almost all interviewers will advise you to keep your focus on solving the obstacles of the hiring company. Also, they'll be looking for you to answer questions about the problems you've resolved for your previous roles, internships, or volunteering efforts.

- The time spent on building a side project can be spent doing other activities, like interviewing at more places, completing an online course, or a masterclass. You could also explore certifications or learning from a mentor in a structured way. Some would argue that these activities can be more helpful in landing a job than building a side project.

Tips on Presenting Your Side Project

The decision to build a side project lies with you. But, if you do choose to build one, here are a few tips for you to make them work for you in an interview:

- Show don't tell. Put the project somewhere that the interviewer can pull up during the interview to see what you have done. This could also mean putting the app on your own device or taking your wireframes or PowerPoint slides with you, to the interview.

- A mention of your side project can be useful, but you shouldn't explain it unless the interviewer asks you to do so. The same goes for showing the project; show them only when they ask you for it and make the presentation clear but concise.

- In some cases, sending the link to the project along with a thank-you email after the interview can also work. But be mindful that you are welcoming scrutiny of your work, so be ready to receive feedback if they choose to send it your way.

- Don't show something half-baked or something you never showed to anyone else. At least two peers should review your side project, and if it is an app, have multiple people actively using it. These people should be sending you regular feedback. If asked, speak confidently about your strategy for prioritizing and implementing feedback from your peers or the users.

As discussed, there are multiple paths towards this role, but all of them require commitment and consistency from you. You will need to spend time learning new skills and refining the ones you already have. Finding ways to connect with the right people for work and learning opportunities show initiative and passion. Being strategic about this transition is the only way forward for you.

Action Items

Here are some actionable items for you which could prove to be extremely useful at this stage of your career pivot journey:

- Join a few online communities related to Product Management; start spending a couple of hours every week there, reading the content and connecting on the forums. Also, contribute and interact with other members. Connect with people and identify the ones you would like to have as your peers or mentors.

- Run a search for the best Product Management courses and certifications. Shortlist at least two that you can pursue in the next few months. Look for something that matches your schedule, learning style and is within your budget. If you are new to online learning, consider starting with something free and then move onto a paid program.

- Identify at least one skill that you know will help you land a PM job and create a roadmap to master that. You can draft it on paper or even on an online tool. Make sure you follow it and keep it up to date.

- Decide on building, or not building, a side project. Whatever you decide, make sure your decision is based on a well-reasoned rationale. Run a poll or post a question in the online product communities about side projects and their effectiveness.

Chapter Takeaways

- There are multiple paths you can take to move into a product management role. Be creative and strategic about the steps you take for finding opportunities.

- There are multiple levels of a Product Management role, and each has a different set of roles and responsibilities. The higher you go, the more strategic the role becomes.

- Find a tribe and a mentor to help you with your journey. Building meaningful relationships is the only way to get ahead.

- Building a side project is not for everyone, and it doesn't always help you land a job. Consider this thoroughly before you start investing your time.

SECTION II

PREPARING TO PIVOT

Step 2: Find the right company and prepare for an interview!

3

INSIDE THIS CHAPTER

- ☑ **Swiping Right for the Right Company**

- ☑ **Tips for your PM interview**

- ☑ **Tips for a remote interview**

- ☑ **Questions to Ask Your Interviewer**

- ☑ **Action Items**

- ☑ **Chapter Takeaways**

Preparing for the Product Manager Interview

> **"**
>
> *The art of communication is the language of leadership.*
>
> James Humes

This chapter will cover the preparation you need to do before attending a Product Management interview. This work is fundamental; it will allow you to put your best foot forward during the interview, to ensure that you get invited for a second interview, and eventually get a job offer.

Often, companies will conduct multiple interviews with the same candidate to evaluate them, both for technical skills and for ensuring that they are a cultural fit. In most cases, you will be informed about the interviewer's name and position beforehand. This means you can look them up online and get to know them before the interview so that you will be well-prepared.

You can find relevant job listings on popular job boards, Product Management communities, and social and professional networking sites. When you apply for a position, make sure your application is professional and your CV is up to date. Also, ensure everything you say or share is aligned with your goal of getting a Product Management position.

Swiping Right for the Right Company

Not all companies will be a good fit for you and your skills. Also, every company is looking for a different type of Product Manager. Shortlist some product-focused companies you would like to work for and get to the research. You can use search engines, product management communities, professional networks, and review sites to get the required information.

Questions to Ask Yourself When Researching Companies

When you do get to the interview stage, the research you have done will be crucial in helping you explain what you know about the company you are interviewing with and score huge points. The following questions will help you build a complete profile of the businesses that you are interested in:

1. Do they have a professional website and an active social media presence?
2. How does it feel to you? Formal? Playful?
3. Have they been in the news recently? What was it about?
4. Have they raised any funding for any of their products?
5. Does the company already have Product Managers?

6. If yes, can you find them online? Do some research into their education and backgrounds.

7. What does the company sell? Do research on their entire suite of products.

8. Look for reviews of their products, customer base, and current market share in their targeted industry.

9. What kind of content does the company put out? Do they have a blog or a YouTube channel? Check out their product demos and communication.

10. Who are their competitors? Is the company doing well when compared to its competitors?

11. What is their vision, mission, and purpose? Does it speak to you?

12. Who are the people on top? Are they well-liked in the industry?

13. Can you find the company on review sites? What do their current and previous employees say about them? What is the common thread in all the negative and positive reviews?

14. Do they have their finances available online? If yes, look at them.

15. Can you find details on their employee perks and facilities online? Check them out as well.

Once you spend some time gathering this data, you will get some sense of the company's status and future trajectory.

If the company doesn't have any Product professionals, I wouldn't recommend joining them, as they will expect you to build processes around Product Management. This will be a lot to handle, and your chances of failure are likely to be higher. Instead, find a company that already has a few Product Managers; you will learn from their experiences by working closely with them. There will also be a Senior Product Manager at the workplace who you should seek out and make a proposal for them to mentor you.

Companies do look for specific backgrounds for their Product Management candidates, depending upon their products and industry. Some companies, like Amazon or VMware, search for technical Product Managers. Like Facebook or Airbnb, others will search for more all-rounder Product Managers who are both tech and business-savvy. Finally, some companies prefer Product Managers from mainly business backgrounds, like Salesforce. The roles and responsibilities of all these different types of Product Managers will vary, and each company will have its own set of expectations from its Product Managers. Look for a company that aligns with your skills, background, and goals for better growth.

If you can find your interviewer(s) online, see if you can find common ground. For example, a shared alma mater, shared interests, friends or acquaintances, or a previous employer, etc. This will help you in making a connection during the interview. Whether they offer you a job or not, make sure that you build new relationships during this journey. Always seek to expand your network and never burn any bridges.

Tips for your PM interview

Product Management interviews are detailed and focus on both the skill set and the personality of the candidate. Here are some tips for your upcoming Product Management interview:

- Prepare some notes on the company's Product (s); your thoughts, ideas, questions, and some improvements you can think of. The same goes for their competitor products.

- Prepare some notes on your favorite Product or a few products in different categories. This discussion is common in Product Management interviews.

- Prepare your career stories on problem-solving, leadership, failure, prioritization, and team management. These must be real experiences. Think about your journey, whether as a professional or student, and prepare a brief narrative to demonstrate different professional abilities.

- If you want to show a side project, have it ready to display, be it on a device or in the form of a hard copy.

- You can take notes during an interview, but I would suggest that you stay focused on the interviewer. You can always collect your thoughts and take notes once you have a few minutes to yourself after the interview.

- Prepare a few thoughtful and open-ended questions for the interviewers. These should be about the specific role, the company's culture, as well as their current and future trajectory. Almost all interviewers give you time to ask your questions. Utilize this time to get to know the people and the company better.

- Say thank you; always send a thank you note or email, along with any follow-up questions or answers within a day, after the interview.

Tips for a remote interview

Onsite interviews are usually the norm, but with the changes in work cultures around the globe, remote interviews are becoming common. Here are some things to do when preparing for remote interviews:

- **Prepare the environment:** You need to find a quiet and undisturbed corner, a table and chair, good light, and a neutral background.

- **Do a test run:** Make sure your equipment is working correctly, including your laptop, camera, microphone, earphones, internet, etc. Have a backup plan, if possible.

- **Download the virtual meeting app:** If you are attending an online interview, performing a test run on the app a day before the interview will make you feel more confident, and you won't have to look for features during the interview.

- **Turn on the 'Do Not Disturb' (DND) feature:** It distracts you and your interviewer to see notifications in an interview, so make sure your DND feature is on. This will be found in your operating system settings.

- Keep yourself muted while the interviewer is speaking, and don't open other tabs or apps during the interview.

- Remote interviews give you an opportunity to share your screen and show your projects and work samples. Utilize this opportunity to the fullest.

As with other interviews, the most critical aspect in a PM interview is your ability to focus, understand the questions, and respond to them comprehensively and succinctly. When it comes to behavioral or strategic questions, make sure you pause for a moment, formulate at least an outline of your answer, and then respond. For these questions, you are required to demonstrate your abilities and thoughts by using storytelling, along with the clear context of the problem. Your answer should follow the SAR method *(The SAR Method for Product Management Interview Questions, 2020).*

- **Situation:** The problem being discussed along with the context.

- **Action:** What you did to solve the problem in each context.

- **Result:** What happened after you performed the action(s).

This will help the interviewer gauge your ability to work through real-world problems and challenges. Also, they will see how you articulate your thoughts and opinions in a structured way.

Another important aspect of interview preparation is to spend some time in self-reflection by understanding your own goals and motivations. An interviewer will ask you questions about who you are as a person. They will want to know your unique traits, strengths, and weaknesses, and you should know how to answer these questions. Work on understanding your preferred communication style and work patterns. Also, explore different ways of learning to see which one works the best for you. This ability to self-reflect will help you in interviews and your future career as a Product Manager.

You should also stay updated with the latest technology and business news by subscribing to relevant online publications. Keep an eye on the latest developments in the industry and the companies you like. I'm a regular reader of VentureBeat, Mashable, TechCrunch, and HackerNews. You can check these out or find others that you enjoy reading. This will help you keep your finger on the pulse of the ecosystem, giving you the most current knowledge to reinvent yourself.

Questions to Ask Your Interviewer

At the end of every professional interview, you will usually be given an opportunity to ask any questions about the company's role or the company. This can be an excellent way to clarify details about the position, get to know the company, and better understand the product team. It would help if you prepared a few strategic and thoughtful questions beforehand, and these shouldn't be questions that a simple Google search about the company can answer.

I am listing down a few as examples for you, but please feel free to create your own list.

1. Can you describe the current composition and organization of the product team? What has evolved over time?
2. What is the leadership style followed by the executives and senior managers?
3. What is the overall communication style within the organization? How often teams meet and share progress?
4. Who determines the product strategy? Who can impose changes to the product strategy? Is there a single owner of the product strategy?
5. Who defines Product KPIs and Metrics? What are

the current KPIs and Metrics?

6. How does the leadership acknowledge and celebrate individual and team contributions?

7. What type of skill up and growth opportunities are available for the teams? Do you have a formal mentoring or leadership program?

8. What is the company's risk appetite?

9. How is failure handled within the organization? Is it punished?

10. How often do team members receive formal feedback on their performance?

11. What would you expect me to deliver in the first 30 days?

You can see these are open-ended questions that tell you about the inner dynamics of the organization and the product team. You need this information to decide on whether or not you want to join the company, should they offer you a position.

An interview is a learning opportunity for both parties, and asking the right questions is a win-win for both. By being actively engaged and focused, the interviewer will determine your ability to ask meaningful questions and construct thoughtful answers.

Action Items

Here are a few exercises from this chapter for you. Be sure to complete these before moving ahead:

- Create a list of at least the top five companies you like, and see yourself working there as a Product Manager. Make sure you choose these companies after answering the research pointers from this chapter. Rate the companies and prioritize your list. Keep this list for future use.

- Search online for some general interview questions and practice your answers in front of a mirror or with a friend. You can go the extra mile by recording yourself and then reviewing it later to check areas for improvement.

- Find and subscribe to at least two relevant publications and spend at least an hour every week reading interesting stories and news there. Explore publications specific to technology products and the business world.

- Watch a few videos online related to general and Product Management specific interview tips and tricks. Make a list of all the suggestions that are new to you. You can also write a blog post about it to help other people.

Chapter Takeaways

Find yourself the right company by spending time researching and learning about them before and during the interview.

- Prepare yourself for both on-site and remote interviews by following the tips in this chapter.

- Use the SAR method to answer the contextual questions asked by the interviewer(s).

- Asking thoughtful questions of your interviewer can leave an excellent impression and give you the desired insights into the company and its product team.

SECTION III

CRUSHING THE PRODUCT MANAGER INTERVIEW

Step 3: Ace your PM interview by mastering your understanding of key product management areas!

4

INSIDE THIS CHAPTER

☑ **What is an Elevator Pitch?**

☑ **Tips on Delivering a Better Elevator Pitch**

☑ **Elevator Pitch Examples**

☑ **Learn to Sell Yourself**

☑ **Action Items**

☑ **Chapter Takeaways**

Hacking the 'Elevator Pitch'

> **"**
>
> *Think like a wise man but communicate in the language of the people.*
>
> *– William Butler Yeats*

I am confident that you've already identified and applied to a few of your desired companies at this stage. You've probably also heard back from them! In almost every interview, you'll get an opportunity to present an elevator pitch in front of the interviewer(s). They won't explicitly ask you to sell yourself or give an elevator pitch; instead, this will come in a question asking you to introduce yourself.

This question is an opportunity for you to make a case for yourself and convince the interviewer you are the perfect match for this position and for this company.

In this chapter, we will be exploring the topic of creating an excellent elevator pitch. I will also share a couple of brilliantly presented elevator pitches from which you can learn.

Let's dive in!

What is an Elevator Pitch?

An elevator pitch is a snapshot of who you are, what you do, and your professional aspirations and goals. It is usually less than a minute long, given in less than 150 words. Professionals use elevator pitches all the time, in networking events, career fairs, and while giving job interviews.

It is called an elevator pitch because it reflects the idea that you can talk about yourself or your Product in the amount of time it requires you to share an elevator ride with a prospect. The ideal time duration varies from 30 seconds to 2 minutes, but we will talk about how to deliver one in 60 seconds for the purposes of this text.

An elevator pitch delivered in an interview doesn't reiterate whatever is already on your resume. Instead, it gives an interviewer the ability to get to know the person behind that resume. The pitch shouldn't focus on your previous roles or work history, rather on your skills, qualities, and aspirations. It is also a conversation starter, so your elevator pitch should intrigue the interviewers, and they should be asking you follow-up questions about your skills and experiences.

Tips on Delivering a Better Elevator Pitch

In my years of interviewing candidates for various positions, I have heard a few excellent elevator pitches. But there were also many average efforts, and unfortunately, way too many disorganized ones. Here are some pointers that will help you avoid being in the last two categories.

- **Don't give an impromptu elevator pitch:** It is the conversation starter, so don't wing it. Make sure you have practiced it multiple times in front of an audience.

- **Don't rush it:** Your goal is to make the other person understand what you are saying. Make sure you speak in a natural tone and a moderate voice.

- **Don't talk like a robot:** Smile. Speak pleasantly and politely while making eye contact with your audience.

- **Please don't create a one-size-fits-all elevator pitch:** Create versions of it depending upon the occasion and the audience.

- **Don't make it longer than a minute:** Sixty seconds is the hard cut-off.

- **Don't make it a bundle of jargons or buzzwords:** People can see right through a flaky elevator pitch. Make it as simple and as authentic as possible.

- **Don't start with your work history:** Start with who you are. Focus on your aspirations and unique characteristics.

- **Don't create pitfalls for yourself;** Make sure you don't mention things you wouldn't want to explain in a follow-up question.

- **Don't copy from other people:** You should let your creativity shine in your elevator pitch.

- **Don't include the company values:** Even though some people may advise you to do so, no matter how hard you try, it will end up looking forced and tacky.

- **Don't start a pitch unprompted:** Let them ask you, and then you can begin.

Elevator Pitch Examples

I am sharing a couple of excellent elevator pitches that I have heard while conducting interviews for a mid-level Product Management position. They have, of course, been modified with names and places changed, but they remain helpful examples of what "good" looks like. Read them multiple times and see if you can write something along these lines for yourself.

Elevator Pitch Number 1:

"Hi! My name is Maria, and I am an accountant-turned-designer-turned-product manager. My skill set is mostly user experience-centric, and I want to work with a functional and aesthetically pleasing product. I love interviewing, observing, and interacting with users and enjoy experimenting with user experience to increase customer retention and sales. I enjoy taking pictures, and my goal is to work on a product that is targeted towards creatives like myself."

Elevator Pitch Number 2:

"Hi! I am Gitte, and I have recently relocated to London from Denmark. I have my first degree in technology and the second one in business strategy and have nearly five years of experience in Product Management. I enjoy reading in multiple languages and have a keen eye for data and behavior patterns. I am currently working with a team remotely to build a machine learning app for differently-abled folks. My goal is to become a product accessibility expert."

You can see the brilliance of these elevator pitches; they are concise, straightforward, engaging, impact-focused, and clearly give you a snapshot of the person. They have not mentioned their entire work history. Instead, they have focused on their skills and qualities and shown how their unique personalities and experiences can add real value to the organization that hires them. There are also some leads for follow-up questions in these pitches, which they have deliberately added so that the listener would ask them further questions.

I asked Maria the following:

1. How can we increase sales by improving user experience only?
2. How can we delight our users?
3. What will be the strategy to improve the falling retention rate of an app like Pinterest?
4. What if I offered her a job in a company that makes business apps for accountants?
5. Does she have a photoblog? Can I see it?

For Gitte, I had the following questions:

1. What made her think about being an accessibility expert?
2. What other domains or industries has she worked in?
3. What are the best strategies to analyze user behavior patterns?
4. What problem does her current Product solve for differently-abled people?
5. What languages does she know? Which one is her favorite?

These elevator pitches tell us more than what is usually written on a resume; they are specific to work and touch upon the interests, value system, and personality traits of a candidate. You should present yourself as human and the type of person the company is looking to hire.

Learn to Sell Yourself

Interviewers also ask other related questions that will allow you to sell yourself. You can see some examples below:

1. Why should we hire you?
2. Why are you the right person for this job?
3. How can you add value to this company or Product?
4. Describe yourself in five words.
5. How do your peers, or your best friend, describe you?
6. Tell us about your best and worst personality traits?
7. What are your strengths and weaknesses?
8. How would you define your work ethics?
9. How would you define your leadership style?
10. How would you define your communication style?

Questions like these gauge who you are and decide if you are the right fit for the organization. They also help to understand your creativity in answering tricky questions with tact and authenticity. As mentioned earlier, an elevator pitch is a conversation starter, so if the start is a bit shaky, it may give your interviewer an unfavorable impression of you, so make sure you work on multiple versions of an elevator pitch and practice them regularly.

Action Items

And now, time for some to-dos. You know our usual drill:

- Create an elevator pitch for the following occasions, keep the audience and your objective in mind while writing these, and make sure that you use less than 150 words for each.

  » An interview for an entry-level product management position with the hiring manager

  » An introduction with a possible mentor to advise you on a future move to a big-five or startup company

  » Meeting new people at a networking dinner, where everyone is given a minute to introduce themselves to the group

- Deliver these in front of your friends and family or record yourself. Find time to do some work on your choice of words, voice, and delivery.

- Ask a peer or a mentor to review your elevator pitch and give you feedback. In return, offer to help them with their elevator pitch. Make it a win-win for both of you.

- Create and finalize an elevator pitch for your next Product Management interview. Rehearse it as much as you can.

Chapter Takeaways

- You will be asked to present an elevator pitch in an interview. This will be your first moment to shine, and you should make it a conversation starter.

- Prepare yourself by creating a few versions of an elevator pitch for yourself. The content and tone should depend on the context and audience for your elevator pitch. Be authentic and ensure that it reflects who you are as a person.

- Prepare answers for possible follow-up questions that may probe you about your personality. Sell yourself to the interviewer but don't make it a bland or cheesy sales pitch.

5

INSIDE THIS CHAPTER

- ☑ **What is Product Strategy?**

- ☑ **Five-Whys**

- ☑ **Types of Customers**

- ☑ **Types of Product Businesses**

- ☑ **Product Strategy Questions**

- ☑ **Answering Product Strategy Questions**

- ☑ **Product Strategy Questions to Practice**

- ☑ **Action Items**

- ☑ **Chapter Takeaways**

About the Product

> **"**
>
> *The essence of strategy is choosing what not to do.*
>
> – Michael Porter, World-Renowned Economist and Business Strategist

Now you are ready to move onto the Product Management focused part of the interview. The most common questions asked during an interview like this are around product strategy, which includes building new products, improving the existing ones, reinventing something for a new use case, etc. Most of these questions don't have a right or wrong answer, but the purpose of these questions is to ascertain how the candidate thinks and solves a challenging problem.

This chapter will tackle questions around product strategy and how you can prepare for this part of the interview. I will decode and solve a few questions and then leave you with some examples to practice, along with a list of action items.

What is Product Strategy?

A product's strategy is about achieving the Product's business objectives and finding a workable plan to make it happen. Specific questions need to be answered when coming up with a product strategy; What are the user personas? What are the challenges being solved? What are the company's goals for the Product? These questions gauge your ability to verbalize and articulate your thoughts around strategy, prioritization, decision-making, analytical thinking, and creativity.

Before we start working through a few questions, let's talk about the target audience or target users. These are the people who can get the best use out of your Product, and they are the ones you have in mind when strategizing and designing your Product. We are looking to grab and retain their attention, providing them with enough motivation to spend money on the Product. Every Product has a target audience. These may contain different personas with different demographics, but the user base will share a somewhat similar problem that our Product will solve for them.

Every Product should be an answer to a question, a solution to a problem, or an improved way of doing something meaningful. Let's look at Dropbox. The concept is not entirely new, but it provides a better way of storing and sharing files and working collaboratively. So, all these software products around you are either solving new real-world problems or, in some cases, finding ways to improve the existing methods of getting something done.

Another aspect to consider is your Product's ability to grab the user's attention and get them hooked so that they keep coming back. This is called user retention, and almost all products want this more than anything else. They need new users and want the existing users to spend more time on the Product, which means more user engagement. We want the products to be 'sticky,' which means we need repeated use by the users and the Product's ability to seep into their daily routines and become a part of their lives.

This can be achieved by actively listening to your customers and working closely with different product functions to improve the key product features and launch new practical features based on their business value and impact.

Five-Whys

This is an interrogative technique designed to identify the root of a problem. It's mostly used in the engineering, technology, and consulting industries. It was developed and refined by Toyota Motors, and they use it for their trouble-shooting processes.

This technique is used in Product Management interviews where an interviewer may question your assumptions. They are clarifying questions about a problem. Using 5-whys can foster critical thinking, creative problem solving, and innovation in product teams. This technique is popular in Product Strategy questions and will help you logically unpack your thought processes. The idea is to start with first asking the fundamental question of "why" the problem is occurring, then four follow-up questions of "why," which should eventually funnel to the real root of the problem.

Types of Customers

Customers can be classified in multiple ways, but the following is how we broadly categorize them while thinking and strategizing about our Product:

- Early adopters.
- Loyal customers.
- First-time customers.
- Customers that stopped paying you.
- Customers of your competition.

While answering Product Strategy questions, you can ask your interviewer about the category or categories of customers that are of interest to them. This can help you scope the question and respond in a way that aligns with your interviewer's intentions.

Types of Product Businesses

There are usually four types of product businesses. Each Product will fall either in one of the following or in a variation of these:

- **Business to Business or B2B:** in this case, the trade happens between two business entities, where one is the customer of the other. An example of this can be Alibaba B2B Marketplace.

- **Business to Consumer or B2C:** here, the trade happens between a company and its consumer, which is usually the end-user. An example of this can be Amazon.

- **Consumer to Consumer or C2C:** in this business type, consumers trade with each other, primarily online. An example of this can be Craigslist.

- **Consumer to Business or C2B:** in this modern business type, consumers create value, and the business consumes it. An example of this can be influencer marketing platforms.

You must include the items above as part of your clarifying questions.

Product Strategy Questions

During the interview, you will be asked questions about redesigning, relaunching, improving, expanding, or even reinventing a product.

I am listing down some questions for you. I have asked some of these myself as an interviewer, and a few of them have been thrown at me whilst being interviewed. I can also tell you that there is at least one question on the list that tripped me up. Bonus points if you guess that one correctly.

1. What if you were the CEO of Airbnb? What would you do differently?

2. How would you relaunch Facebook to improve its market share and image?

3. Name your top three most used products and why you use them so frequently?

4. How would you design a social network for realtors?

5. How would you monetize a multilingual recipe-sharing website?

Answering Product Strategy Questions

You can clearly see a pattern here. These questions are tough; the answers wouldn't be at anyone's fingertips.

They're also purposefully vague, so the best way to start with a question like this is to ask clarifying questions and build a baseline understanding of the problem and its objectives.

You are expected to create and share a framework to ensure that the solutions you present are structured and don't seem chaotic. Once you are clear on the specific objective of this question, you can generate ideas. For example, if the question is about designing a social network for realtors, you may ask why a realtor would want to connect with another realtor? Will they find value in a product like this? Do they have a specific monetization strategy in mind, etc.?

Before we start brainstorming, let's confirm what the interviewer is looking for. They want a framework from you. For example, if we want to monetize a recipe-sharing website, we can either have the users pay for the access or the advertisers pay for the ad space. This serves as a boundary for the ideas, and we can now start listing factors down that can help us achieve our already established objective.

The next step is to evaluate the solutions or ideas we have generated. It's likely this will start with a discussion with the interviewer on recognizing the feasibility, trade-offs, and alignment of a certain idea with the product strategy. Let's look at two from the examples above:

- For the realtor app example; Sharing information by integrating a forum could be a reason to make connections on the social app, but you should conversely ask; do realtors like to share information? In most cases, no. Unfortunately, that would mean that this idea doesn't respond to a market need, so it wouldn't be included in your development recommendations.

- For the recipe-sharing app example; You know that FMCGs and businesses in the restaurant industry would be interested in pushing their ads there because it would suit some of their target markets. This idea would also work for big grocery stores and fitness-related products. Based on this quick analysis, you can see the idea seems to have some merit, and you would recommend that it be explored further.

The whole conversation should also be structured, and you should evaluate each idea based on the initially agreed-upon problem, your knowledge about the product itself, the domain, as well as the target audience.

The last part is about concluding this discussion by recommending at least one solution that can help us achieve the objective and is feasible to implement. Here you will produce your final answer to the question. For example, when asked: How will you increase the average watch time per user on Netflix? Your answer should sound something like this: To increase the average watch time of an individual user, the better strategy is to improve the recommendation algorithm. This generates recommendations based on their watch list and search history, their interest in different genres, and their given ratings. We can improve this by getting user feedback on our recommendations and verifying if they click, watch, or complete the shows or movies recommended by the platform algorithm.

For questions around your favorite apps and creating a rationale for your opinion or feelings for this app, or even finding ways to improve an app, you need to do this exercise with friends, family, or peers and see what you come up with. Thinking about something on the spot and then deriving a strategy around it can be daunting. Instead, prepare and work on some practice questions before going for an interview.

Product Strategy Questions to Practice

Here are a few questions for you to think about and practice.

1. How would you design an alarm clock for a blind person?
2. Why would you choose YouTube over Vimeo?
3. What's your most favorite productivity app? How would you improve it?
4. What is your most favorite product in entertainment, and why?
5. How would you prevent trolling on Twitter?
6. How would you build a product to buy and sell preloved office furniture?
7. How would you redesign Goodreads?
8. If you could invent the ability to teleport small objects, how would you monetize this invention?
9. If everyone gets free and unlimited bandwidth of the internet, what would you build and why?
10. What should be Instagram's product strategy for the next five years?
11. How would you find out the product-market fit?
12. How would you approach competitor analysis?
13. Tell me about any company that has excellent Customer Experience. How would you define

their strategy?

14. Suggest a new feature for Facebook. Give a rationale for your answer.

15. How would you know if a Product is well-designed?

When practicing these questions, list the clarifying questions for each of the above, and then create assumptions to work through the problems. See if you can follow the same steps as I have explained above. Identify areas where you are not convinced and restart the thinking and structuring process. Use pen and paper to work on these problems and avoid using the internet to search for anything. Also, use a kitchen timer to put a 5-minute limit to each question.

Domain-specific questions are also popular. Interviewers will ask you about the previous domains or industries you are familiar with if they match their product. They may ask you to do some analysis, or if there is nothing similar, they may ask you to draw parallels.

Action Items

- Practice the above questions and see if you can discuss some of them with your peers and mentors. This can happen in person or online and can help you grade your own answer and think through the problem. Writing your answer down and getting it reviewed can also be helpful.

- Reflect on your previous experience and draw on some strategy examples from other domains and industries. Use them strategically in your answers to highlight your unique exposure and ability to connect the dots. Start a discussion around this in one of the Product communities or forums. Observe the unfolding discussion and see what you learn.

- Do some research on unmet user needs and see if you can identify an area where a solution is much needed. Create some notes on the solution you would like to build and launch. Think about the features, users, strategy, and other related elements. Show it to your peers, hear their thoughts and see if you can improve your idea and convert it into a side project.

- Practice building UI sketches or wireframes. You can do it for an existing application or for a new idea. Find a tool that you like and spend at least a few hours on it.

Chapter Takeaways

- Product Strategy questions usually don't have right or wrong answers and serve the purpose of understanding the problem-solving ability of a Product Manager.

- Be prepared to explain your thoughts and ask questions to clarify the actual question and its intended objective.

- Learn to use five-whys and prepare yourself to answer repeated whys from the interviewer without losing your chain of thoughts.

- Working through a problem requires structure and the ability to generate creative ideas and then finding merits or flaws in them for further consideration.

6

INSIDE THIS CHAPTER

- ☑ **Estimation Questions**

- ☑ **Methods for solving Estimation Questions**

- ☑ **Build your own Cheat Sheet**

- ☑ **Answering Product Estimation Questions**

- ☑ **Product Estimation Questions to Practice**

- ☑ **Action Items**

- ☑ **Chapter Takeaways**

Estimating like a Pro

> **"** *Be stubborn on vision, but flexible on details.*
>
> – Jeff Bezos, founder and CEO of Amazon

This is the chapter that will require the most amount of time and attention from you, as estimation questions are the hardest questions asked in a Product Management interview. These questions are designed in a way to throw you off balance, but a competent candidate will shine through this section of the interview. Finding the precise answer is not the goal here; instead, it is about working through incomplete data and solving problems in a step-by-step manner.

In this chapter, we will explore the types of estimation questions, patterns for solving them, and then build a cheat sheet. I will guide you through some possible solutions to a couple of estimation questions and leave you with a few to practice on your own.

Estimation Questions

Estimation questions, also known as 'Fermi's Questions', are defined as "making estimates and using mathematics to answer a question. In more colloquial language, they might be termed 'back of envelope' calculations" (Fermi problems, 2019). These are used in interviews in multiple professions, like engineering, technology, consulting, and marketing. A few examples of Fermi's questions are listed below.

1. How many bald people live in the US?
2. How many Rubik's cubes will you need to fill a stadium?
3. How many grains of wheat are in a 5lbs bag?
4. How many gallons of water is in Lake Michigan?
5. How long will it take to drive to Mars if it were possible?

Estimation questions are a critical component of Product Management interviews and are of three major types.

Market Sizing Questions

These questions are asked to estimate the market size for a product or service. Market size is usually defined as "the total number of potential buyers of a product or service within a given market, and the total revenue that these sales may generate." (Market Sizing – Estimating Product Potential, n.d.). The questions help establish a Product Manager's approach to estimating a product's market size when there is no concrete data available. It is also to gauge your ability to analyze key factors and make clear assumptions to reach an answer.

Here are a few market sizing questions:

1. How many airplanes take off from Dubai Airport each day?

2. How many pounds of French fries are sold each year in Canada?

3. What is the market size for prescription eyeglasses in China?

4. How many people buy organic produce in the US?

5. How many dog walkers are in New York City?

Revenue Estimation Questions

As the name suggests, these questions are related to the annual revenue of a current or upcoming product, service, or business.

1. How many bottles of moisturizers are sold per year in the US?

2. What is the annual ads revenue of Facebook in Europe?

3. How much money did Bank of America make in 2020?

4. How much money does a YouTuber make in a year?

5. How many smartwatches are sold in China every year?

Guesstimate Questions

All other types of estimation questions belong to this category. This entails guessing the answer to a vague question and is related to approximation and estimation. You should reach a number at the end and explain your assumption and process on the way. Here are a few guesstimate questions below:

1. How many trees are there in South Africa?
2. How many gallons of water are used in all the hotels in Italy?
3. How many birds migrate each year?
4. How many children are needed to have a mass the same as a dinosaur?
5. How far can you run in a year if you run for 8 hours a day?

Methods for solving Estimation Questions

Estimation questions can be approached in different ways, but the two most used methods are top-down and bottom-up. Both approaches should lead to a similar answer, but you will find that one will be easier to use than the other, depending upon the problem.

Top-down

Here, you will start with the largest number and then break it down and refine it to reach your answer. An example of this could be identifying the number of people who would watch your video tutorial on growing a home garden. You will start with the largest number possible, which will be the total number of internet users around the globe. Then refine it for language and region, and then investigate how many of them would be interested in a gardening video.

Bottom-up

Here, you will start with the smallest number. So, for example, the question is the average yearly revenue of a company selling real Christmas trees in the US. You will start with the cost of one tree, the number of people who celebrate Christmas, and the percentage of people who would buy an actual tree, and so on.

Build your own Cheat Sheet

A cheat sheet is a list of facts and figures that can be used to work out solutions for product estimation questions. Building your own can bring confidence, swiftness, and accuracy to your answers during an interview.

A basic cheat sheet should have both local and global facts and figures. Below is a comprehensive but not exhaustive list of data points you can find online and add to your cheat sheet:

1. The world's population
2. The population of the different continents.
3. The population of different countries (e.g., US, UK, China, India, Japan, etc.)
4. The population of major cities around the globe (e.g., New York, Mumbai, Paris, Tokyo, etc.)
5. The number of households in various countries
6. The total number of smartphone users around the globe and in various countries
7. The total number of internet users around the globe and in various countries
8. The interest rates in various countries
9. The average global life expectancy
10. The average number of people per household in various countries
11. The median household income in various countries.

12. The financial inclusion rate in various countries

13. The poverty threshold in various countries

14. The literacy rate in various countries

15. The average WIFI bandwidth.

16. The average CTR for a search ad

17. The average landing page conversion rate

18. The average file size for a smartphone camera picture

19. The average file size for a 90-min 720p movie

20. The average cost of per GB mobile data

21. The average cost per GB storage

22. The average cost of a smartphone

23. The average cost of a computer

24. The yearly revenue of big-five tech companies

25. The total users for the big-five tech companies

This, I believe, will help you in answering estimation questions, but you can add more facts to this list. I don't recommend having too many, as memorizing facts is not the goal here. Instead, you are learning how to solve a problem by building a framework and creating clear assumptions.

Answering Product Estimation Questions

The next thing to look at is the structure or framework for answering product estimation questions? Here is what I use, and you can use the same or create your own version.

- **Ask questions;** you need to create a scope for the problem by asking questions to further clarify the context. In most cases, interviewers do answer these questions, and in a few cases, they may ask you to create your own assumptions
- **Break it apart;** you will need to create a flow for answering this question, and the flow should be logical. Choose a pattern, either top-down or bottom-up.
- **Make Assumptions;** write down your assumption, both about the problem and the numbers.
- **Calculate;** use round numbers to easily do mental calculations. Practice basic math problems to get prepared for this part.
- **Gut-check;** see if your answer sounds right. For example, the average number of active users on Facebook in the US shouldn't be larger than the country's population.
- **Debrief;** assess your assumptions and answers, then discuss them with the interviewer. This will show them your ability to analyze and make adjustments where necessary.

Let's break down the following example question.

What is the market size of body washes in the US?

Let's start with the first step and ask clarifying questions:

1. Do we include both medicated and cosmetic body washes?
2. Are we also including shower gels in this category?
3. What is the size of an average body wash bottle?
4. Do we include baby products in it?

I will answer the above questions for you:

1. Yes
2. Yes
3. 400 ml
4. No

The second step is breaking it down further. For this, I am choosing the top-down approach because the original question is about the market size. I am also making the following assumptions:

- Only the adult population uses the body washes
- The adult population is 75% of the total population
- The entire adult population takes a shower once a day
- All of them use some sort of cleansing product
- Out of all the adult population, 50% of them use body washes
- One person uses five, 400ml bottles of body wash a year
- One body wash is priced at 5 USD in retail

Now, let's calculate.

- The US population size is 320 million people.
- 75% of the adult population showers every day and uses some form of cleansing product: 240 million people.
- 50% of them use soap, and the other use body wash: 120 million.
- An average person uses five 400ml bottles of body wash a year: 120 million * 5 = 600 million.

- An average body wash bottle of 400ml costs approximately $5: 600 million * $5 = $3 billion.

When I gut-check this number, it looks like an underestimate to me, as the global market is over $40 billion, and the US is the biggest consumer in this category. We need to refine the above assumptions and recalculate to see if we can arrive at a more probable result.

Let's take another question and try to follow the same process.

How much revenue does Samsung earn by selling smartphones each year in the US?

Below are my assumptions:

- We are only including smartphone sales, excluding accessories and other smart devices
- We are including sales for new phones from Samsung and not taking any resale activity (if it happens) into account
- People change their smartphones every year
- The average price of a Samsung phone is 300 USD without insurance
- 50% of smartphone users use Android phones
- 30% of Android users use Samsung phones
- 80% of Americans have smartphones

Let's calculate.

- The US population size is 320 million people
- 80% of them use smartphones: 256 million people
- 50% of them have Android phones: 128 million

people
- 30% of them buy Samsung phones: 38.4 million people
- The average phone price is $300: $11.5 billion
- People change their phones once every year, so $11.5 billion is their revenue in sales per year

We can further refine this by improving our assumptions and asking more clarifying questions about the problem. The above structure is straightforward and gives us clarity while working on a vague problem. When answering these questions, never put forward a final number to your interviewer without first explaining your process.

Product Estimation Questions to Practice

Now use the following questions for practicing your estimation and approximation skills:

1. Estimate the number of motorbikes required to start a motorbike-sharing operation in Mumbai, India.

2. How many pairs of rain boots are sold worldwide?

3. How many avocados are consumed in Mexico every year?

4. How many house plants are bought each day in the US?

5. How many people have a driver's license in South America?

6. What is the annual revenue of TikTok in South Asia?

7. How many windows are there in Paris?

8. What is the annual revenue of 3-star hotels in Vegas?

9. How many pairs of Old Navy jeans are sold in a year?

10. How many chickens are sold in the US each year?

11. How many white Maruti Suzuki cars are in India?

12. How many messages are exchanged on WeChat in an hour?

13. How much money is spent on medical insurance every year in New Zealand?

14. How many women are online right now globally?

15. How much money is spent on buying basic groceries in the US?

Be sure to do a sense-check of all your answers and try to find the actual data online. See if it matches your estimated answer.

These questions help interviewers determine if you possess the following abilities:

- Ability to structure your answers in a logical way

- Ability to ask the right questions and reflect your understanding in the solution given

- Ability to work with numbers quickly and accurately in your head or on paper without using any devices

- Ability to formulate and communicate ideas and opinions about the context of the problem and its solution

Action Items

- Build a cheat sheet for yourself and memorize it. Make sure you add both local and international facts and data points to it. You can also ask your peers and mentors to review it or share theirs.

- Practice the above questions by creating a written structure and making clear assumptions about different data points. Write down your answer, see if this data is available online and if your estimate is close to what is available online? If yes, good job. If not, how can you improve your process of calculations?

- Practice the above questions by both top-down and bottom-up methods. See which one is the easiest to follow for each of these questions.

- Practice some basic math operations for mental math, like multiplications, divisions, percentages, and ratios. Also, time yourself while practicing mental math exercises.

Chapter Takeaways

- Estimation questions are an essential part of the Product Management interview process that can help the interviewer evaluate your logical and analytical thinking capabilities.

- Estimation questions are of three types, market sizing, revenue estimation, and guesstimates. You can work on them by following either top-down or bottom-up methods.

- Building and memorizing a quick cheat sheet can be helpful during an interview for pulling out facts and figures from your memory.

- Working on an estimation problem is a step-by-step process and requires you to follow a clear approach, with explicit assumptions and quick and accurate calculations.

7

INSIDE THIS CHAPTER

- ☑ **Types of Technical Questions**

- ☑ **Tools to Explore**

- ☑ **Answering Technical Questions**

- ☑ **Technical Questions to Practice**

- ☑ **Action Items**

- ☑ **Chapter Takeaways**

Let's Get Technical

"

What new technology does is create new opportunities to do a job that customers want done.

– Tim O'Reilly, founder of O'Reilly Media

Understanding and working with technology is one of the most important skills for a Product Manager. You should communicate with ease with your engineering teams and advise them on technical issues whenever required.

This portion of the interview will evaluate your understanding and expertise in available technologies out there. The interviewer is not looking for a coding expert but rather a generalist who understands how tech works and can build algorithms to solve real-world problems.

This chapter contains the details on different types of technical questions, along with a list of some of my favorite Product Management tools. I will also be working through a few technical questions for your learning, and as always, it will end with a list of practice questions.

By the end of this chapter, with some practice, you should be able to answer most technical questions in a Product Management interview!

Types of Technical Questions

Primarily, there are three types of technical questions asked in Product Management interviews. These questions help the interviewer evaluate your ability to work with technology tools and understand and explain technical concepts and functions.

Explanation Questions

This is about explaining how technology works. Interviewers ask these questions to see if you know how a certain technology works and can explain this in layman's terms to people without the technical knowledge. These questions sometimes follow with, explain X to your grandma, or a 5-year-old, or to your mom, etc.

Some example questions are:

1. How does the internet work?
2. Explain bitcoin to your grandma.
3. How would you explain Stripe to a 5-year-old?
4. How does Google Analytics work?
5. Explain the technology and business model behind Facebook.

Algorithm Questions

In Computer Science, an algorithm is a finite sequence of well-defined, computer-implementable instructions that typically solves a class of problems or performs computations (What is an Algorithm, 2020). These questions are asked to allow you to demonstrate your ability to solve problems by creating patterns and step-by-step instructions.

Some examples of these questions can be:

1. How would you design an algorithm to change the file formats of image files?
2. Design an algorithm to detect the shortest route between two cities, Los Angeles to San Francisco.
3. Write an algorithm to detect spam emails.
4. Design an app that counts your steps and estimate calorie burn.
5. Design a security feature for the Venmo app.

Miscellaneous

All other questions will fall under this category of technology questions. This may include describing your previous experiences with technology teams, your ability to speak and understand 'techno-ese", and your favorite tools and tech stacks.

Some example questions are:

1. How have you previously dealt with technology challenges? How did you work with non-technical stakeholders on this?
2. How comfortable are you with managing an engineering team?
3. What is your favorite tool for wireframing?
4. Have you ever designed a technical solution? Tell us about it.

5. Have you ever tested a tech product? What did you look for in it?

Tools to Explore

Product Managers use several tools for doing their jobs effectively and efficiently. I would like to share some of my favorite tools in different categories that have made my life as a Product Manager easier. As a beginner in Product Management, you are not expected to be an expert on all of them, but you should know how to use a few of these excellent tools.

- Communication Tools: Zoom and Slack
- Collaboration Tools: GSuite and Microsoft 365
- Customer Feedback Tools: SurveyMonkey and Google Forms
- Wireframing Tools: Figma and Balsamiq
- Project and Task Management Tools: Jira and Asana
- User Experience Tools: HotJar and Adobe Target
- Analytics Tools: Google Analytics and Pendo
- Product Roadmapping Tools: ProductPlan and Roadmunk
- Presentation Tools: Canva and Prezi
- Mindmapping Tools: Xmind and Freeplane
- Screen Capture Tools: Screencastify and Snagit
- Software Documentation Tools: ReadTheDocs and GitHub
- A/B Testing Tools: Google Experiments and Optimizely

Answering Technical Questions

When answering a technical question, be sure to explain it by using simple terms and no jargon. You will not impress the interviewers by compounding the complexity of the concept. Explain things simply and solve problems by following a structured approach. You should ask clarifying questions, explain thoughts by following a step-by-step process, and provide a summary at the end.

Let's start with an explanation question.

How does Scrum work?

You can explain it as follows:

Scrum is a methodology used by teams to achieve their goals. The project is divided into fixed-length time boxes, such as one week or two weeks, and the team is expected to finish a set of features or work items in that time box. Each task is iterative, so the team will build upon their previous outcomes and complete the project quickly.

It has a small team size so that communication overhead can be minimized, and the team meets daily to discuss their process and challenges. Scrum is used in all sorts of industries, like software, automotive, marketing, and consulting. It is flexible and can be used for projects of all sizes and complexities. Scrum can also be used alongside Kanban, a method for a visual representation of the workflow.

At this stage, the interviewer may ask you questions about your explanation. For example:

- You mentioned that a time box could be 1-week

or 2-weeks. Why is that? Can we make a bigger timebox, say of 3 months?

- How does it help in completing the project quickly?
- How long is the daily meeting?
- What is Kanban? How do we use or implement it?

You should be able to answer all these follow-up questions.

Let's take another technical question now.

How does WhatsApp work?

The explanation could look like this:

WhatsApp is an app for both iOS and Android smartphones that facilitates its users to send text and media messages over the internet and deliver audio and video calls. The messages are encrypted, so hackers can't get into it, and the encryption key is changed for every new conversation to ensure maximum security. WhatsApp uses an open protocol called Extensible Messaging and Presence Protocol (XMPP) for data exchange.

It is specifically designed for instant messaging and contact list maintenance. XMPP is decentralized, secure, and flexible and can be used to send and receive messages both in one-on-one conversations and in group chats. Whatsapp offers to back up your messages using your cloud service and sends push notifications to your phone.

This explanation will open the opportunity for the interviewer to ask you follow-up questions around

XMPP and encryption, etc. They may also ask you about synchronous or asynchronous communication.

Let's look at an algorithm question now.

Design an algorithm to find even numbers.

This one is simple. Your response should be:

I would take a number and divide it by 2. If the remainder is 0, the number is even; if not, the number is odd.

How about this one?

Design an algorithm to find the area of a circle.

The response here is:

The area of a circle is calculated by Pi * Radius * Radius. We know the radius, and the value of pi is universal. We will take radius as input and set the value of pi at 3.14. Apply the formula by multiplying pi by radius twice, and you have the area of a circle.

The interviewer could then ask you what would change if the radius were not available and only the diameter is? You should solve this by responding that you can find the radius by dividing the diameter by 2.

You could also be asked about your favorite tool stack for different workflows.

What are your favorite tools for communication and why?

An excellent response for this question might be:

I enjoy using Slack for text conversations and Zoom for team meetings. Slack is easy to use, and the user interface is uncluttered. You can use it as an invitation-only platform for the product team, which is great, and the mobile app is as efficient as the web interface.

Zoom is easy to use, and the ability to attend a meeting without signing up is excellent. It requires less bandwidth and has advanced features, like attendee mode and breakout room. Zoom is excellent for handling meetings with many participants or for an online event.

The demand for Product Managers who are competent with technology has been growing steadily. This tells us that a career in Product Management requires sufficient proficiency in technology and the ability to communicate in a language understandable for all stakeholders. This may require you to change your language and use of terms depending upon your audience.

Technical Questions to Practice

- What are your favorite tools for facilitating communication and collaboration?
- What do you know about SaaS, PaaS, and IaaS?
- How does Cloud technology work?
- What is meant by server-side and client-side?
- Design an algorithm for minimizing wait time at the doctor's office.
- What is the difference between open-source and proprietary technology?
- What agile methodologies have you worked in? How does Kanban or Test-driven Development work?
- How would you optimize the storage for Dropbox? Design an algorithm for this.

- How does blockchain work?
- Design an algorithm to detect fraudulent credit card transactions.
- What are full-stack, MEAN stack, and MERN stack?
- Name a few cloud technology platforms. What are their features?
- How would you design the database of Google forms?
- How does RESTful API work?
- What is meant by Emerging technologies?

Technology is constantly evolving, and the knowledge of a Product Manager should also evolve with it. Keep yourself up to date by reading about the latest technologies and talking to people who develop technology for a living. Ask intelligent questions and establish a peer-learning relationship with people in this sector. Playing around with no-code and low-code frameworks can also help in understanding technology concepts.

Action Items

- Answer the above questions verbally by using a 3-minute timer and recording yourself. Check your answers online and see if you have explained them correctly. Try to explain it to people without much exposure to technology, listen to their feedback, and use it to improve your explanations.

- Work on algorithm exercises and pay close attention to your logic. See if you can identify multiple ways of solving a single problem.

Consider which method you will pick and why? Can you build some quick patterns for yourself for solving algorithm exercises? Talk to a mentor about it.

- See if you can find a good online course on 'Introduction to Information Technology' or similar and complete it. Also, look for products based on emerging technologies. Research the underlying technologies and see if you can explain them in under 3-minutes to someone who doesn't belong to the technology industry.

- Find the list of different tech stacks online and compare their similarities and differences. Familiarize yourself with them and learn a bit more about the background and features of different languages and frameworks.

Chapter Takeaways

- Good Product Managers understand the technologies they are working with and can communicate well with technical and non-technical team members and stakeholders alike.

- Interviewers usually ask three types of technical questions: explanations, algorithms, and miscellaneous.

- Ask clarifying questions before solving a problem and use a structured approach for your solutions. Make sure to prepare for follow-up questions.

- Tools are an important part of a PM's job. Familiarize yourself with a few of them before going into an interview. Having familiarity with a few of them can be advantageous to you in the process.

8

INSIDE THIS CHAPTER

- ☑ **Understanding Product Metrics**

- ☑ **Understanding KPIs**

- ☑ **A/B Testing**

- ☑ **Answering Product Measurement Questions**

- ☑ **Product Measurement Questions to Practice**

- ☑ **Action Items**

- ☑ **Chapter Takeaways**

Analyzing the Metrics

“

*My biggest regrets are the moments that I let a
lack of data override my intuition on what's best
for our customers.*

– Andrew Mason, founder of Groupon

Measuring the health of your product is an essential
activity of a Product Manager's role. You need to 'lean
in' to the data; to discover what is working and what
requires more improvement. This analysis acts as
a window to your product's future and can help you
predict the correct course of action.

In this chapter, we will discuss product metrics and
Key Performance Indicators (KPIs). By learning how
to decode different metrics, you will find the most
valuable insights and be able to answer questions on
these topics. At the end of the chapter, you will find a
list of questions to help you practice.

Let's get into it.

Understanding Product Metrics

Product metrics are quantifiable data points that a Product Manager tracks and uses to gauge the success of its product. Examples of product metrics include conversion rates, churn rates, and monthly recurring revenue tracking. These metrics should all come from the measurement part of the product strategy (What Product Metrics Matter?, 2021).

Metrics are used to make better-informed decisions for a product, including the strategy and utilization of the team's time and given budget. We also use metrics to gather buy-in from stakeholders on a specific course of action. They are valuable tools to learn more about your product's performance and help us improve the product by focusing on valid metrics.

What would you do if your metrics are moving in the wrong direction and are unstable? As a Product Manager, you are required to investigate and use the data to inform your decision. You can keep improving the feature, pivot from the original plan, or 'grandfather' the feature entirely.

Not all metrics are suitable for all products. They are also dependent upon the industry, your business model, and your Product's objectives. So be careful when choosing your top metrics. Keeping an eye on them should be one of your daily tasks.

A few examples of Metrics can be:

1. **Session Duration;** The amount of time a user spends on the app or website performing some activity. The session duration ends after a set time of inactivity from the user.

2. **Daily Active Users;** Number of active users per day.

3. **Traffic;** Visitors going into the app or website, both organic and paid.

4. **Bounce Rate;** Ratio of people who left the app or website after only seeing one page or screen.

5. **Net Promoter Score;** Number of people who will likely promote your product in their network.

Vanity Metrics

Vanity metrics are metrics that make you look good in front of others, but don't help you understand your product's performance in a way that informs future strategies (What are vanity metrics? n.d). An example of this can be the number of downloads. This number can appear meaningful, but if the ratio of users who sign up for the app is poor, the number of downloads tells us nothing about the product's performance.

The same is true for measuring the number of signups but not measuring user retention. Many people may sign up for your app, but are they actively using it? The latter is more meaningful to measure.

Understanding KPIs

Key Performance Indicators or KPIs are measurable values that show you how effective you are at achieving your product's objectives. KPIs are different from Metrics, as Metrics simply track the status of a specific feature or factor but don't tell us about the status of our product objectives (Taylor, J. 2020).

The most used KPIs are listed below:

1. **Sales Revenue;** The amount of money coming in via product sales.

2. **Customer Acquisition Costs;** This refers to the money spent on attracting a customer. It includes all sales, marketing, promotion, and operations activities.

3. **Customer Churn;** Number of users who stopped buying your product or paying for the subscription.

4. **Customer Satisfaction Score;** How satisfied are your customers with your products? It is usually measured on a scale of one to five.

5. **Customer Lifetime Value:** Amount of money a user will spend on your product throughout their lifetime.

A/B Testing

An A/B test is used to determine which version or variant of something will perform more effectively in the market (A/B Test, 2020). It is also called 'split testing' and is used by Product Managers to decide on UI elements, and user flows and find the optimal version of it. This is done by using automation tools, which perform controlled experimentation on your product.

We divide our traffic by showing them different variations of the same page or screen and compare the patterns of how users are engaging with each of them. Here, two options are compared, which have subtle changes to avoid alarming the users. Usually, the first or 'A version' is the control version, and the second or 'B version' is the variation.

A/B Testing generates excellent data points, which can be used to measure the best ways to show or approach a certain element or feature in the product.

Answering Product Measurement Questions

In a Product Management interview, you will be asked about Product Metrics. Remember, the interviewer is looking for an answer that is well thought through and given after scoping the question and explicitly verbalizing your assumptions.

Let's work on a question related to Product Measurements.

> *How would you improve the average order value of a high-end fashion brand's e-store?*

We can create our list of assumptions here or ask questions, whichever is more suitable. Your answer might be:

My assumptions are:

- The current order value is $500, and we want to push it to $625
- The brand sells clothing items and accessories
- The brand never offers any seasonal discounts
- The brand offers bundle packages
- The brand also sells limited edition items

As a Product Manager, I would test out the following strategies:

- Offering quick or free shipping on a minimum order value.
- Showing the buyer other items that go well with

what's already in their cart. An example of this would be, recommending a piece of accessory to go with a dress.

- We can also bundle products by selling a beach bag with a pair of sunglasses.
- Increasing the prices of each item can also achieve a bigger order value.
- Set up a customer loyalty program; the customer could have access to limited edition items upon exceeding a specific order size.

You would then go through each strategy and discuss the pros and cons with the interviewer. When working as a Product Manager, you may pick up a top two or three strategies to test out, as testing all of them can be a cost and effort-intensive activity.

Let's look at another question.

If you are a Product Manager for a dating app, what will you measure for your app?

You might respond with the following:

Here are my assumptions:

- The app is used by adults only and is for finding long-term relationships.
- The app makes matches on interests, personality traits, and location.
- The app is available for all users, and anyone can start a conversation if there is a match.
- The app is free and has no monetization for now.

Below is the list of measurements that I will be interested in:

- Daily/weekly/monthly active users
- Number of matches per week
- Number of matches per user
- Number of conversations per week
- Number of conversations per user
- Number of swipes per day/week/month
- Number of swipes per user
- User retention
- User churn
- Net Promoter Score (NPS)

We can further refine the answer by creating assumptions or asking questions about the context. If the app is paid service based, sales revenue will also be an important measurement.

Product Measurement Questions to Practice

1. How would you increase the average watch time per user on Netflix?
2. How would you improve the completion rate of an online course?
3. How would you measure the success of Facebook reactions?
4. If you are the Product Manager at Pinterest, how would you measure user retention?
5. Your user retention is dropping every day, and you have seen this trend for over two weeks. Do

you think this is the right time to inform all the stakeholders?

6. What is the most important metric for Trello, and why?

7. How would you set goals for UberEATS?

8. Should YouTube autoplay videos by default? What metric will help you decide in making this decision?

9. You see a drastic change in the number of people signed up to your job board this month. What do you think is the cause? How would you test your hypothesis?

10. Your sales revenue is dropping, but the number of new free sign-ups is increasing. What would be your strategy to investigate this situation?

11. If you are a Product Manager at WhatsApp, how would you measure the success of WhatsApp stories?

12. What are the key metrics of an eCommerce business?

13. How do you define success for a personal finance app?

14. What are the most relevant product metrics for the Google Calendar app?

15. How would you increase user retention in Jira?

In this part of the interview, you are being evaluated on how you identify and analyze data points. This then links to how you connect this information to the product strategy and its key objectives. These interview questions are used to gauge both critical and analytical thinking and your ability to understand business cases.

Action Items

- Work on the above practice questions and see how to break down a problem. Write down your assumptions and try to get your answers peer-reviewed.

- Look for analytics tools online. Identify the ones that companies most use. If a free version or trial is available. Get yourself familiar with it.

- Watch Suhail Doshi's talk on How to Measure Your Product, which is available on YouTube. Take notes and make sure to revise them before your Product Management interview.

- Repeat the above process for Adora Cheung's talk on How to Set KPIs and Goals. Also available on YouTube.

Chapter Takeaways

- Product metrics are used to measure the health or status of a launched product. We set these metrics to identify areas of improvement and learn more about our users.

- Vanity metrics add no value to a product discussion, and a Product Manager should be careful when selecting these metrics for their Product.

- KPIs are used to measure our Product's objectives. They use metrics but have set goals for each performance indicator to gauge the success or failure.

- A/B testing is performed by splitting the user traffic, showing them slightly different versions of the app or website, and observing and making conclusions based on user response.

9

INSIDE THIS CHAPTER

- ☑ **Product Business Models**
- ☑ **Pricing Strategies**
- ☑ **Economies of Scale**
- ☑ **Answering Product Pricing Questions**
- ☑ **Product Pricing Questions to Practice**
- ☑ **Action Items**
- ☑ **Chapter Takeaways**

Getting Pricing Right

> " *Price is what you pay. Value is what you get.*
>
> *- Warren Buffett, chairman of Berkshire Hathaway*

Pricing the product is about recovering the product's cost and making a profit but also about selling it at a price that makes sense to the customers. The value they get out of it must exceed the money they spend on it.

Product Managers work with their business teams to find the right business model and pricing strategy for their product. They aim to put a price tag on it, which doesn't break the bank for the user yet builds substantial and repeated revenue for the company.

In this chapter, we will learn about product business models, along with some common pricing strategies. As in the previous chapters, I will guide you through a couple of questions to enhance your understanding of the topic and then leave you to work through the practice questions.

Product Business Models

Product business models can be broadly classified into

four main models. Each model has further variations, and Product Managers can work through them to find the right fit for their product.

One-time License Fee

In this model, customers pay a one-time fee for the product and then use it for a lifetime. This is an older model and works well for products, where a repeat sale is unlikely. It also costs more upfront, as the customer is paying for the product only once. Most traditional desktop and standalone software applications are sold using this model. The model poses a higher risk to the consumer, as there is a higher upfront cost and creates vendor lock-in. An example of this is Scrivener, a word-processing program for writers.

Subscription Fee

This means charging customers a monthly, quarterly, or yearly fee for the use of the software. The subscription model is most compatible with Software-as-a-Service (SaaS) solutions and is one of the most used business models for technology products. There is usually no upfront fee, and customers pay a small amount periodically with an option to cancel the subscription anytime they want. Most SaaS solutions also give users the ability to import and export their data, so the vendor lock-in isn't as great a concern as with the previous model. An example of this is Microsoft 365, the SaaS version of Microsoft Office.

Free with Ads

With this model, users pay nothing for using the application but are shown ads to generate revenue. Advertisers are charged per view, per click, or per impression for their ads. This is also a commonly adopted model, especially for social media sites. The biggest example of this is Facebook, with roughly 86 billion US dollars in revenue in 2020.

Transactional

Here, the customer pays per transaction. This model usually works for financial technology applications, as well as for affiliate models. The fee can be a fixed amount per transaction or a percentage of the total amount. An example of this is Stripe, an online payment processing company.

Other variations of the above models include:

1. **Freemium**; Customers use the product for free but pay for the premium features.

2. **Per-User;** Customers pay for the number of users in their organizations.

3. **Per Usage;** Customers pay for the usage, for example, the amount of data stored in the cloud.

4. **Demo;** Customers can only see a demo after requesting it and then buy the product using a one-time license or a subscription model, whichever is made available.

5. **Free Trial;** Customers can use the product for a limited number of days and then buy the product, using a one-time license or a subscription model, whichever is available.

6. **Freemium with Free Trial;** Customers can use the product for free but can check out the premium feature, by utilizing the free trial of premium features, for a limited time.

7. **Tiered Pricing**; This is a subscription model, with multiple tiers available, to purchase according to the customer's needs.

Pricing Strategies

Product teams usually think in terms of the following Pricing Strategies.

1. **Cost-plus Pricing;** Simply calculating your costs and adding a mark-up.

2. **Competitive Pricing**; Setting a price based on what the competition charges.

3. **Value-based Pricing;** Setting a price based on how much the customer believes what you're selling is worth.

4. **Price Skimming;** Setting a high price and lowering it as the market evolves.

5. **Penetration Pricing;** Setting a low price to enter a competitive market and raising it later *(How to price your product, 2020).*

Choosing the right product strategy depends on the type of product and its context, which includes competitors, strategy, target users, and so on. For most modern products, you will observe value-based pricing is used as a strategy. You will put a price tag on each differentiating feature of your Product and then arrive at a price that works for you as well as for the customer. In this win-win-based approach, the customer should be the bigger winner by getting the most value out of your product.

Economies of Scale

The economies of scale refer to savings caused by increased production levels. In other words, a good economy of scale means that the more of a product a business makes, the more cost-effective production becomes (Tech economics: scale and scope, 2019).

This works brilliantly in software solutions, as the cost for making a copy of your software is negligible when you compare it with the cost of developing the software initially. Tech Products can easily achieve economies of scale, especially when it comes to SaaS products. With the use of cloud technology, iterations of the software are created automatically and without human intervention, which makes them even cheaper.

Answering Product Pricing Questions

Let's jump right into a couple of product pricing questions. The same framework applies here that we have looked at in other response examples previously; ask scoping questions and explicitly state your assumptions.

Can you think of a case where increasing a product's price added more to the number of licenses sold?

Here are my assumptions:

- It is a software product.
- Licenses are both one-time and subscription.
- Licenses are available for anyone to buy.
- The product has competitors in the market.
- The product has some value to its customers.

Below is what I think would work as a response:

This can work in cases where your competitor's prices are high and you are selling at a more cost-effective pricing strategy to enhance your product's market penetration. This can backfire, as your users may consider your product to be of low quality or come with poor support. It also depends on how you package your product. In some cases, re-bundling the product and increasing the bundle price can add more to the sales. This can work well, but for a specific context of a product.

You can further improve this answer by refining your assumptions or getting into specific examples.

How do you know what your customer is willing to pay when you don't have any direct competitors?

My assumptions are:

- It is a software product.
- Licenses are both one-time and subscription.
- Licenses are available for anyone to buy.
- The product has some value to its customers.

You can test out multiple pricing strategies here. Either price skimming or value-based pricing is appropriate for this example.

A price skimming strategy could work, as there are no direct competitors. You can set a higher price and watch how customers react to it. It will also set a higher price bar in customer's minds, so you won't have to lower your price by much. However, this can also be dangerous, as competitors could spot an opportunity and sweep in by setting a lower price. They could hijack your market share by targeting customers who are reluctant to pay a higher fee.

For value-based pricing, you can perform market research and check in with current customers and prospects to determine how much they are willing to pay for the product. Another alternate exercise is to see how much cost and time savings customers are experiencing by using your product.

Check in with the interviewer and get their feedback to see if your answer is aligned with their thoughts. This is a thinking exercise, so you shouldn't give a number without justifying the reasons behind it.

Product Pricing Questions to Practice

1. What business model and pricing strategy should you pick for an ERP system targeted towards consulting firms? Why have you chosen this strategy?

2. How do you know what your customer is willing to pay, when you don't have any direct competitors?

3. If I decide to monetize WhatsApp, what business model and pricing strategy would work best?

4. Is freemium the best model for all communication apps? Explain your answer.

5. How should I react to my competitor increasing their prices?

6. If the price doesn't work, should I lower it to meet customer expectations? Is this the only strategy?

7. How do you think Microsoft came up with a price

for Office 365?

8. Is offering a discount a good strategy for a gaming product? Explain.

9. What's the best way to create subscription tiers for a dating app?

10. How much should you charge for drone-based delivery of food?

11. How should you ease your customers into an increased subscription price?

12. If you launch a SmartWatch competing with Apple's watch, how much would you price it?

13. Should we take credit card information from a user while giving them access to a free trial account? Justify your answer.

14. Do you think pricing something at USD 4.99 instead of USD 5.00 has a real impact on sales? Why or why not?

15. What are the pros and cons of the transactional model?

You need to have a certain level of business sense and knowledge to work through these questions. As a Product Manager, you should have a good understanding of consumer psychology to help you rightly price your product and generate substantial sales.

Action Items

- Work through the given list of practice questions; using the same process described in this chapter. Discuss them with your peers and mentor, if possible.

- Research and identify competing products in the

following categories and find out their business models along with their pricing strategies.

- Communication products.
- Personal Finance products.
- Marketing Automation products.

- Discuss your findings from the above exercise by writing a blog post and sharing it with your Product Management peers and mentors. Ask them for their feedback.

- Start a conversation about the Economies of Scale with a peer. Compare notes on your understanding and see if it adds up to your current knowledge.

Chapter Takeaways

- Product pricing requires thorough research and experimentation to see what price tag works for your customers, as well as for you.

- There are four main business model categories: transactional, subscription, one-time license, and free with ads. Other available models are a combination of these four.

- There are five broader pricing strategies for software products, and each has its own set of pros and cons

10

Your PM Persona

> **"**
>
> *At the end of the day, your job isn't to get the requirements right — your job is to change the world.*
>
> *– Jeff Patton, Veteran Product Manager and Consultant*

Your persona is another way of describing your behavioral traits. Behavioral questions are asked in interviews to learn more about the personal skills of a professional. These are usually asked in a way that the interviewee will have to describe a scenario and bring in some previous experiences to the table for discussion.

This chapter will contain the core behavioral traits required for Product Managers, types of biases, and a section with some sample questions. You will also find practice questions and a list of action items at the end.

Most employers will have a list of behavioral traits that they are looking for, that they believe will help propel the businesses' products forward. Behavioral interview questionss help a candidate to show these skills to their future employer, ensuring that both parties are a good fit.

Let's get into it!

Core Behavioral Traits for PMs

Adaptability

This means the ability to respond to change quickly by learning new skills and making quick but sound decisions. You will find yourself having to adapt to an ever-changing market and user needs. You must also have the agility to learn as you go and solve problems at a moment's notice. Circumstances will change rapidly, so this is one of the most sought-after behavioral traits in a Product Manager. You will be required to learn, decide, push, or pivot, whatever is the best solution for the situation.

Self-Awareness

This means knowing yourself by being aware of your traits, behaviors, biases, and feelings. It is an excellent trait, as it teaches us to be self-disciplined and keep an open mind about new ideas and challenges to our way of thinking. It also helps in stemming our biases and tendency to stereotype. A self-aware person is usually a better leader who learns from their mistakes and knows when it's the right time to pivot.

Leadership

Every Product Manager is a leader, as they must rally their team to build something of value, usually within a limited time and budget. They need to create a vision and make sure that everyone feels committed to that approach. This is a tough job and requires proven leadership abilities, like integrity, empathy, the ability to communicate and influence. A Product Manager should also delegate to their team but be confident enough to know when to trust or question their judgments.

Result-Oriented

This is the Product Manager's ability to prioritize which results, work items, or data points are more important than the others. They stay focused on achieving the outcome with the highest priority, depending upon the product's strategic objectives, and plan for the steps to be taken to reach those goals. A result-driven Product Manager is said to be one of the greatest assets of a company.

Conflict Resolution

A Product Manager must work with several stakeholders and teams, and the potential for conflict in this situation is almost inevitable. The Product Manager must have an openness to listen and collaboratively find a workable solution when conflicts arise. This requires the ability to empathize, appease, and negotiate with all parties involved. Conflict resolution also requires self-awareness and the ability to influence.

These are the behavioral traits that you need to be a successful Product Manager, and the interviewer will also be looking to see if you demonstrate this during the interview. Take a minute to see if you already have these traits and any action you can take to cultivate or refine them further.

Cognitive Biases

All of us have biases that can cause us to focus on some things and ignore others erroneously. Cognitive biases can prevent us from working at our optimal level, becoming a cause for a lapse in judgment and poor decision-making. As a Product Manager, you should be aware of any biases and keep them in check while making decisions and prioritizing work items. We will look at a few types of biases below.

Affinity Bias

We trust people who are in our circle, or ones we like, and tend to listen to their feedback on our work and priorities. This can be dangerous for decision-making as we need to go outside our affinity circle and talk to people who are actively using the product. Avoiding an echo chamber is crucial for a Product Manager; constant exposure to real-world users helps us avoid our affinity bias.

Confirmation Bias

We are naturally inclined towards data that appear as evidence of our existing ideas or opinions. This can be dangerous, as we will start seeing patterns where none exists. A workaround for this bias is to look at all aspects of the data, setting out your Key Performance Indicators beforehand. Don't change unless you have a logical reason to do so, and keep an eye out for vanity metrics.

Authority Bias

This is when we overvalue the opinions of people who either have a higher status than us or have some form of authority on the subject matter. This is counterproductive as discussions may end up going up and down aligned with the authority figure's opinions and not on facts. Consider that all ideas and discussions brought to the table should be evaluated on their own merit and not based on any role or status hierarchy.

Survivorship Bias

Sometimes we focus on the survivors of a process or a task, people who are already our users, not on the ones who left our product. Learning from the lost users can be beneficial and help us think strategically about the missed opportunities. Build ways to find out the reasons customers leave your product.

Because Product Managers make many decisions about their products daily, they should learn to evaluate their own decisions, by considering these biases.

Answering Behavioral Questions

In this part of the Product Management interview, your interviewer wants to verify your ability to solve problems and articulate your thoughts.

Let's start with an example question.

How would you motivate your team after a major setback?

Here, they want to know about your leadership qualities, so you need to talk about your ability to communicate with your team.

My answer would look like this:

In one of my previous assignments, we launched a feature for our enterprise users. The feature was developed after many requests, and we user-tested it with good results, but we noticed low activity there once we launched it. The metrics confirmed that the users were not that engaged with this feature. I could sense the low morale of my team and had to find a way to motivate them for the upcoming releases.

I did the following, and it worked well.

- I reached out to my key team members discussed the lessons learned from this setback.

- We had a team meeting to discuss this and brainstorm ways to better prioritize and identify business value and impact.

- We took time to reflect and then documented our learnings. We made sure that the document was available for everyone throughout the organization.

- We re-iterated the idea that failure shouldn't be punished and is an opportunity to learn and improve.

- We also did a small team-building activity, and I personally thanked my individual team members for their amazing work.

Be prepared for the follow-up questions on this. This is an example, and of course, your story would differ from mine. Don't fabricate stories; highlight something from your work experience, and make sure you rehearse these anecdotes before the interview.

Let's look at another example:

Tell me about a successful presentation you gave. Why do you think it worked?

The interviewer wants to know what counts as successful in your mind. Also, they are looking for authenticity and self-awareness.

You can talk about:

- The subject matter and your expertise.

- The audience of the presentation and how they engaged with you.
- The goal of the presentation, length, use of humor, logical flow, or simplicity.
- Your ability to handle tough questions.

Behavioral Questions to Practice

1. How creative are you? Explain your answer with examples.

2. How would you break the news of a major budget cut to your team? How would you ensure that they don't get demotivated?

3. Tell us about a time when you resolved a conflict between your team members regarding a feature's implementation approach?

4. What aspects of this career do you find the most challenging?

5. What aspects of this career do you find the most boring? Is there any way you can make them interesting?

6. How do you learn the best? Do you call yourself a quick learner? If yes, how did you reach this conclusion?

7. What is your strategy for reaching out to users or customers?

8. What kind of people do you enjoy working with? What kind of people do you not want to have in your team?

9. Tell us about a time when you made a mistake, and someone corrected you. How did you react? What did you do to fix it?

10. How would you prioritize stakeholder requirements in your product roadmap?

11. Tell us about a time when you had to redo a major portion of your work/product. How difficult was it to pivot when you were nearing your envisioned finish line?

12. You were asked to add a new feature to your current release plan, and you don't have any bandwidth. How would you communicate this? Will you change your release plan or drop a planned feature out?

13. Giving tough feedback is something that every PM must do; what is your strategy to approach this? How would you tell a team member they need to scrap their work and redo it?

14. Why did you choose to pivot to Product Management? What do you bring to it from your previous work experiences?

15. Have you ever built a consensus on something? Was it a good idea? Tell us what happened.

Behavioral questions are an excellent way to get to know the Product Management candidate better and learn the things that are almost never mentioned on a resume. It is based on the idea that someone's past behavior can be used to predict their future behavior.

Action Items

- Work on the above practice questions. Discuss your answers with your peers and mentor, if possible. Be authentic with your answer.

- From the list of core behavioral traits, find the ones that you think you need to work on. Create a mini-list and order it according to importance or your need for improvement. Start with the top trait and create action items to cultivate this.

- Watch Daniel Gross's talk called 'How to Win'. This is an excellent talk on leadership and is available on YouTube. Take notes and write a short summary of your learning from this.

- Find and watch the TedTalk by Simon Sinek called 'How Great Leaders Inspire Action'. Find at least three key learnings and document them. Start a conversation about it with your peers and mentor.

Chapter Takeaways

- Behavioral questions are used to filter out the best candidate for specific work culture and these questions reveal the person behind the resume. The goal here is to find the best cultural fit for the organization.

- The core behavioral traits for a Product Manager are, Adaptability, Self-Awareness, Leadership, Result-Orientedness, and Conflict Resolution. Every Product Manager must possess these behaviors.

- Human beings are intrinsically biased, and we need to be continuously aware of our own biases. The most common types of biases include authority bias, confirmation bias, survivorship bias, and affinity bias.

BONUS CHAPTERS

11

A Product Manager's Mindset

"

Your principles are your true north because they instruct how you will handle every situation, especially when there is no easy choice.

– Brian de Haaff, Co-founder and CEO of Aha!

Learning to get into the right mindset can help us perform better in a Product Management role. It teaches us how to think like a Product Manager by identifying our strengths and weaknesses, as a professional. This role requires us to generate new ideas, constantly evolve them and then test them to find the ones that work the best.

The ideas presented in this chapter are drawn from a talk given by Ken Sandy at a Product School event, and I really enjoyed watching him present this framework *(Video: Think Like a Product Manager, 2017).*

The Four PM Mindsets

There are four PM mindsets that you need to learn to master your craft.

Explorer

This Product Manager is an expert brainstormer with the ability to expand the product by generating numerous out-of-the-box ideas. They build a compelling product vision and never hesitate to borrow ideas from other products. An explorer enjoys pursuing and prototyping multiple feature ideas and can think about goals and advanced features without being bogged down by the implementation details.

Analyst

This Product Manager is a detective. They enjoy following data clues to uncover problems and opportunities. Their focus stays on understanding customers' needs. They set and work with performance metrics and KPIs. An analyst is an expert interviewer and can bring in a new depth to customer interviews by knowing their customers on a very human level.

Challenger

This Product Manager is a natural skeptic, but this can be very helpful. They challenge every observation and opinion to uncover biases and implicit assumptions. They stay focused on finding flaws with the strategy or the product itself and are good with critique and feedback. A challenger is very good with prioritizing and aspires to achieve continuous validation by distilling customer data.

Evangelist

This type of Product Manager is a cheerleader. They know how to communicate well with the team and rally them towards the finish line. They are empathetic and know how to build a strong team that takes ownership of the product. An Evangelist is usually not a micromanager but instead focuses on ensuring stakeholder alignment in all situations.

The Balancing Act

You will almost certainly be better at some of these mindsets than others. Most people will be good at, at least one of them. A great Product Manager has a healthy mix of all four perspectives and knows when to make one more dominant, according to the situation. Ensure that you understand the core ideas and value systems behind each of them. While applying each mindset, you need to be conscious of the biases that can affect your decision-making. Alongside analyzing data for better decision-making, paying attention to your intuition is critical.

This is a process of continuous learning and updating your knowledge base with new information about all aspects of a Product, including market, data, features, users, and competition. Practicing these mindsets can be excellent preparation for starting your career as a Product Manager.

Action Items

- Identify your strongest and weakest mindsets. Create an action list to improve the weaker ones. Your goal should be to learn and practice all four mindsets, so assess yourself regularly.

- Document your learning and see what tools and techniques you are learning along the way while practicing these mindsets. Update your skill inventory with these new learnings.

- Watch the presentation by Ken Sandy and learn more about these mindsets and biases we need to be aware of..

Chapter Takeaways

- The four PM mindsets are Explorer, Analyst, Challenger, and Evangelist. Each of them has its own strengths and value systems.

- An explorer is a dreamer, an analyst is a detective, a challenger is a skeptic, and an evangelist is a cheerleader. All four mindsets are important for a product's success.

- As a Product Manager, you should learn to practice all four mindsets to master your craft and develop world-changing products that your customers will be excited to use.

12

INSIDE THIS CHAPTER

- ☑ **Traditional Software Development Methodologies**
- ☑ **Modern Software Development Methodologies**
- ☑ **Agile Manifesto**
- ☑ **Agile Principles**
- ☑ **Understanding Lean Software Development**
- ☑ **Lean Principles**
- ☑ **Understanding Scrum**
- ☑ **Understanding Kanban**
- ☑ **Understanding DevOps**
- ☑ **Good Software Development Practices**
- ☑ **Action Items**
- ☑ **Chapter Takeaways**

Software Development Practices

> " Computers have no idea what goes on outside of them, except what humans tell them.
>
> – Ellen Ullman, Computer Programmer, and Author

Product Managers are responsible for building, launching, and maintaining technology products. These are products with mostly a major software component in them. Software Development is a vast industry with many practices, both old and new. These practices make up the ways we build and maintain software and how the team members organize themselves and communicate within and outside their team. These communication methods have an immense impact on the delivery and quality of the completed product and are essential tools in the Product Manager toolbox.

This chapter will take a closer look at these software development practices, both traditional and modern. We will also get familiar with Lean, Kanban, Scrum, and DevOps, the leading practices in today's era, and explore some crucial practices around developing valuable software solutions.

Let's get into it!

Traditional Software Development Methodologies

Traditionally, the development process was divided into a series of set phases. The team would work on a specific set of deliverables in each phase, and they would perform activities only relevant to that phase. The software was developed by getting complete requirements from the customers or the end-users and then converting them into working software; alongside various documents and artifacts as part of each phase. Planning was done for the whole project, and Gantt charts were used as a visual tool for showing the workflow.

This most basic traditional methodology is known as Waterfall.

Waterfall

- Here, all the phases linearly follow each other. The phases can be five, six, or seven, depending upon your project's needs. The most basic version will have Analysis, Design, Implementation, Testing, and Maintenance. The later versions will have Analysis, Planning, Design, Development, Testing, Deployment, and Maintenance.

- The model has no feedback loops and has a set of standard deliverables for each phase. The planning is done to make everything predictable, and each phase should be completed before moving onto the next phase. The customer will only see the working software once it has been completely developed, tested, and deployed on the production server.

- This model is straightforward and logical, but real-world software development rarely works like this. There is a high failure rate in waterfall projects as it is heavy on rigid planning and documentation and because it is resistant to change.

- Testing happens at the end, and it makes the bug fixes more expensive. It also has no room for changing requirements, as it locks them in the initial phase.

Spiral

- This is a slightly updated methodology that is risk-driven and has a whole phase dedicated to risk management. It also works in iterations, so the software is built in smaller iterations throughout the development process.

- Here, there are four phases, Determine Objectives, Identify and Resolve Risks, Development and Test, Planning the Next Iteration, and each phase has its own activities.

- The first iteration is a prototype that gets us the proof of concept, and then it goes into building features on top of each other. While planning the next iteration, customers or end-users are involved in collecting feedback. This is to ensure that the solution is moving in the right direction.

- It has a high dependency on risk so is not suitable for low-risk or smaller projects, as it may be expensive to implement and sustain because of the expertise required for effective risk management.

Incremental

- This methodology was originally designed for bigger projects with larger teams where they can be divided into smaller teams and work in parallel. The incremental methodology works on the waterfall principles, but it has prototyping added to it.

- The software is built in smaller increments and is merged before releasing it to the customer. This works for both the development and maintenance of the software.

- It shortens the release time and uncovers problems comparatively early in the process. You can also prioritize requirements by delivering important or critical features in the initial releases to the customer.

- Integration can cost more and, if not planned, can create high-risk problems. It is also more expensive than the waterfall methodology and requires a bigger team.

All these methodologies have their pros and cons, but software teams needed something that was robust and not resistant to the changing market and user needs. It is important to understand that time-to-market is one of the most imperative factors in a successful product, and the modern software development methodologies precisely address that.

Modern Software Development Methodologies

Modern Software Development methodologies revolve around quick time-to-market, adapting swiftly to change, and short and tight feedback loops. The idea is to start small and adjust on the way to ensure that you are solving the users' problems. The software will be imperfect, with possibly a few bugs, but adequate to provide the end-users some quantifiable value.

Agile Philosophy

- This came alive in the early 2000s, where a group of software engineers built a manifesto to improve the processes around software development.

- The manifesto gained popularity in the technology ecosystem for its simplicity and value-driven approach. Companies and teams started changing their work processes to align with its principles and found that the method helped them deliver better software.

- Later, different methodologies became part of this philosophy, including Scrum, Kanban, and Lean.

- The agile philosophy puts humans at the center of the process, be it the customers or the team building the software. It aims to reduce the communication and documentation overheads and pushes teams to invest in building relationships and implementing transparent communication patterns.

Agile Manifesto

According to the Agile Manifesto, we are uncovering better ways of developing software and, through this work, we have come to value:

- **Individuals and interactions** over processes and

tools

- **Working software** over comprehensive documentation
- **Customer collaboration** over contract negotiation
- **Responding to change** over following a plan

That is, while there is value in the items on the right, we value the items on the left more *(Manifesto for Agile Software Development, n.d.).*

Agile Principles

The founding team also created a list of twelve principles that were the foundation behind the agile manifesto:

- Our highest priority is to satisfy the customer through the early and continuous delivery of valuable software.

- Welcome changing requirements, even late in development. Agile processes harness change for the customer's competitive advantage.

- Deliver working software frequently, from a couple of weeks to a couple of months, with a preference for the shorter timescale.

- Businesspeople and developers must work together daily throughout the project.

- Build projects around motivated individuals. Give them the environment and support they need and trust them to get the job done.

- The most efficient and effective method of conveying information to and within a development team is face-to-face conversation.

- Working software is the primary measure of

progress.

- Agile processes promote sustainable development. The sponsors, developers, and users should be able to maintain a constant pace indefinitely.
- Continuous attention to technical excellence and good design enhances agility.
- Simplicity--the art of maximizing the amount of work not done--is essential.
- The best architectures, requirements, and designs emerge from self-organizing teams.
- At regular intervals, the team reflects on becoming more effective, then tunes and adjusts its behavior accordingly *(Principles behind the Agile Manifesto, n.d.).*

These principles became the 'north star' for almost all modern software development teams, and current Agile-based methodologies align themselves with these principles.

Understanding Lean Software Development

Lean came from the manufacturing industry, where the focus was on optimizing production and the assembly lines to minimize waste of time, effort, and materials. Software development teams later adopted Lean to optimize the delivery time and build a product that was adequate for the customers without any extra or complicated features.

Lean also popularized the concept of Minimum Viable Product, where a team would deliver a product that would solve the basic problems without any extra features to see if it meets the user needs. Once they know that this is what the user wants, they will iterate from there to improve the product and build it for a larger audience with more confidence. *(Lean software development, n.d.)*

Lean Principles

It has a set of principles that are to be followed strictly for producing optimal results. These principles are:

- Waste elimination in the development process
- Amplifying learning by sharing it with everyone involved
- Late decision-making for minimizing the cost of change
- Fast delivery to test the market needs
- Team empowerment for improved decision-making
- Built-in integrity for better customer experience
- Optimize the whole for building a win-win

Waste in the context of Lean means:

- Partially done work or work in progress
- Extra features with no significant impact
- Relearning of concepts, ideas, and tools
- Handoffs between team members
- Waiting of any kind that causes delays
- Context Switching by switching between tasks
- Bugs or defects

Understanding Scrum

Scrum is one of the most used agile methodologies and is used in all different kinds of industries, including software, manufacturing, research, and consulting. It is a time-boxed approach that is lightweight but flexible enough to cater to varying types and sizes of projects.

Scrum limits the team size to a maximum of 12 and has two fixed roles: A Scrum Master and a Product Owner. The first is the evolved form of a Product Manager, and the second is the evolved form of a Business Analyst and User Advocate. Each has a fixed set of responsibilities, and the roles can't be merged.

A Scrum Master has the following responsibilities:

- Coaching and mentoring the team
- Removing roadblocks and ensuring the unhindered flow of information
- Keeping the time-boxes and ensuring that all events happen on time
- Helping and facilitating the product owner in the best interest of the team and the project

A Product Owner has the following responsibilities:

- Creating, prioritizing, and grooming the product backlog
- Clearly communicating the backlog items and answering questions to the best of their ability

The time-box is chosen at the start of the project, and it can be from one to four weeks long. Each time-box is called a sprint and is planned individually by the team. Once chosen, a time-box's duration can't be changed throughout the development life cycle.

Requirements for the project are gathered in an artifact called a backlog. Which are mostly user stories. These are written, prioritized, and managed by the Product Owner, with some help from the Scrum Master and the Product team. Each sprint will have its own backlog, a subset of the main backlog.

Each sprint is locked during the planning event, and the work items can't be changed or replaced. Each one begins with a planning meeting to decide the end goal and deliverable. The team is self-organized and cross-functional and selects their workload themselves. They also do daily meetings to stay aligned and remove roadblocks quickly.

The end result is an increment, a deliverable that can be released to the customer. After every sprint, the team does a self-reflection activity called a retrospective meeting to improve their work processes.

Scrum works using transparency, adaptation, and inspection principles, and the team builds a sustainable pace to deliver good work until the project ends.

Scrum values include the following:

- **Commitment;** Team members individually commit to achieving their team goals each sprint.

- **Courage;** Team members know they have the courage to work through conflict and challenges together so that they can do the right thing.

- **Focus;** Team members focus exclusively on their team goals and the sprint backlog; there should be no work done other than through their backlog.

- **Openness;** Team members and their stakeholders agree to be transparent about their work and any challenges they face.

- **Respect;** Team members respect each other to be technically capable and to work with good intent *(Scrum, n.d.)*.

Scrum teams are known to use Planning Poker as their time estimation technique. It is a technique where the scrum team builds consensus on the time required to build each user story by using a deck of cards, either physical or digital. It is a gamified technique and requires practice to master. The cards are usually marked with the Fibonacci series to show the inherent uncertainty and incorrectness of estimates.

Another popular estimation technique is Work Breakdown Structure. Here, each feature is divided into tasks, and each task is then estimated in hours. Both traditional and modern software teams used this technique.

Understanding Kanban

Kanban is a lean method to manage and improve work across human systems. This approach aims to manage work by balancing demands with available capacity and improving the handling of system-level bottlenecks. Work items are visualized to give participants a view of progress and process, from start to finish—usually via a Kanban board. Work is pulled as capacity permits, rather than work being pushed into the process when requested *(What is Kanban. 2019)*..

It manages the capacity of the team and creates

transparency. The goal here is to minimize the Work in Progress items and improve the workflow. The visual representation can be a physical or digital board showing work in different stages, and each work item will have one owner. The stages of work can be:

- Backlog
- In Progress
- In Test
- Done
- Blocked

Most modern Project Manager software applications use Kanban boards to simplify the workflows and build transparency in team communication. The team is required to create their own policies and definitions, for example, the definition of done or definition of ready, etc. It can be used alongside Scrum or Lean to visualize the workflow, but some teams prefer to use it as a standalone methodology for Software Development.

Understanding DevOps

DevOps is a set of practices that combine software development (Dev) and IT operations (Ops). It aims to shorten the systems development life cycle and provide continuous delivery with high software quality. DevOps is complementary with Agile software development; several DevOps aspects came from the Agile methodology (*DevOps*, n.d.).

It allows the team to automate processes related to building, testing and releasing the software using some modern tools. This was made possible using cloud technology for building, deploying, and releasing the software to its intended audience.

The phases here include Plan, Build, Continuously Integrate and Deploy (CI/CD), Monitor, Operate and Respond to Continuous Feedback.

- Continuous integration means the practice of merging the updated code to the main code repository as quickly as possible. CI has automated test suites that will run on the newly updated repository and will flag any possible issues.

- Continuous delivery lets the code be auto deployed to the test or production environment. You can automate the release checklist, allowing you to push the updated code whenever you want.

- Continuous deployment lets us create a deployment pipeline that is fully automated and doesn't require human intervention. The deployment will only stop if there are any problems.

All the above are part of DevOps. The team's focus is always on writing better code and using automated checks to minimize human effort in releasing software.

Many cloud technology service providers like AWS and Azure have their own sets of tools for facilitating DevOps for software teams. These tools make things easier for the development team by automating much of their manual work. You will also notice the role of a DevOps Engineer replacing the traditional System Admins.

As a Product Manager, you only need the basic information on these topics so that you can communicate effectively with the engineering team. Learning software development and deployment tools are not part of your role and should be left to the engineering team so that you can focus on making your product a success.

Good Software Development Practices

Here are a few good software development practices to remember. You might even hear them coming from your future engineering teams. These are software development practices that help ensure the team is creating something of great value. Learn them, and implement them with your team:

- Communication between the team members should happen without any barriers and should be instantly possible.
- Test early, test often, and keep testing!
- Testing is not a role, rather an activity and should be everyone's responsibility.
- Requirements are better explained or documented visually.
- Software Development is a team sport; we don't need heroes; we need synergy.
- Write correct code, then improve its performance.
- Add code to your comments and make sure they are readable.
- Wireframing will save you a lot of time and headaches.
- If it takes more than 3 seconds to load, it is too slow.
- There is always a way to make the design simpler.
- Users are lazy, don't make them think or work.

- Improve the code by refactoring it, as early as possible and as much as possible.
- User Testing is the best form of feedback.
- A user story completes a single operation. If it is bigger than that, slice it.
- Document your findings and learnings for both successes and failures.
- Quality is everyone's responsibility.
- Quality software is something that has some value to its user, and they are willing to use it and pay for it.

Action Items

- Find the latest version of the Scrum Handbook and go over it at least once. The handbook has been published by Scrum.org and is written by Ken Schwaber and Jeff Sutherland. It is available online for free.

- Learn about User Stories, Backlog, and Sprint Planning by watching some videos on YouTube. You will find excellent content published by Scrum.org and Scrum Alliance. Make notes and document your learning in the form of a blog post. Share it with your peers and listen to their feedback.

- Watch Dr. Jeff Sutherland's amazing talk at Google on Scrum. You will find it on YouTube. He also gave a shorter talk on Scrum at TEDxAix, which is also a great watch. Take notes and share your learning from these talks.

Chapter Takeaways

- Traditional software development methodologies were rigid and required predictability and advance planning for the whole project. They had set phases and deliverables, and the team size can be anywhere from a couple of people to a few hundred people.

- Modern software development methodologies reduce the communication overhead. They allow the limited time of team members to be better used for exploration and early feedback to improve the quality of the software and quicken the delivery time.

- Lean Software Development is based on the lean concepts in manufacturing, and two software engineers developed Scrum to ensure simplified planning and iterative software delivery. Both are excellent methodologies and are widely used and acknowledged by software engineers.

- Kanban is a method used for visualizing and managing workflows. It can be used alongside Scrum and Lean methodologies.

Glossary

100 Product Management Terms

"The single biggest problem in communication is the illusion that it has taken place."

– George Bernard Shaw - Irish playwright and political activist

This section contains the top terms used in the Product Manager's daily activities and Product Management interviews. Knowing these core concepts and work processes is critical, so for that reason, I have included them in this book. Most of these terms are tech-focused but I have explained them as simply as I can. Make sure you review them before going for your Product Management interviews.

100 Product Management Terms You Should Know

1. **Acceptance Criteria:**

   Conditions that a product should meet to be accepted by its customers. Mostly used in Scrum alongside user stories.

2. Accessibility:

Designing a product in a way that it can be used by everyone, regardless of their abilities.

3. Agile:

A philosophy of getting work done by implementing an iterative model and using small team sizes.

4. Alpha Testing:

A final round of end-to-end testing performed within the organization.

5. Amazon Web Services:

A cloud service platform providing multiple services to customers in the cloud ecosystem.

6. API:

Application Program Interface, a set of routines and protocols for building and connecting multiple software components.

7. Automated Testing:

Using automated testing tools to test software for faulty or abnormal behavior.

8. Avatar:

An icon representing a user over the internet.

9. Backlog:

An artifact in Scrum that has all the user stories.

10. Backlog Grooming:

An activity where the backlog is cleaned and reprioritized as per the changing requirements.

11. **Benchmark:**

   A standard or goal set by a company or product team.

12. **Business Agility:**

   A business that can adapt quickly to changing market and user needs.

13. **Business case:**

   The justification for implementing an idea or a feature.

14. **Business Continuity:**

   Ensuring that the business goes on as per usual, even after an incident or a disaster.

15. **Business Intelligence:**

   Use of tools to transform data into insights for decision-making.

16. **Business Model Canvas:**

   A template for innovating new business ideas or documenting the existing ones.

17. **Burn-down Chart:**

   Represents the amount of work daily, in a sprint or time-box.

18. **Beta Testing:**

   The final round of testing with a sample size of product users before launching the final version.

19. **Call-t0-Action:**

   A link, button, or banner on a website or an app, asking users to take an action.

20. **Cannibalization:**

Competing with another product made by your own company.

21. **Cloud Technology:**

It provides information technology infrastructure as a service to individuals and businesses, including computing, storage, and tools.

22. **Code Repository:**

A central storage place where all your application code is stored.

23. **Content Management System:**

A framework used for managing all types of content for an application.

24. **Continuous Improvement:**

An ongoing process of improving all or any aspects of a business.

25. **Conversion Rate:**

The percentage of product users that take an action desired by the business.

26. **Cost of Delay:**

It is a project prioritization framework helping businesses in qualifying the impact of time on project completion.

27. **Cross-functional Team:**

A team with people having different expertise and belonging to different organization functions.

28. **Customer Advisory Board:**

    A group of customers taken onboard for advising on product strategy and roadmap.

29. **Customer Experience:**

    Interactions of a customer with your business's product and/or services.

30. **Data Center:**

    A physical facility to keep and maintain technology infrastructure.

31. **Data Mining:**

    The discipline where large amounts of data are analyzed to identify patterns and gather insights.

32. **Definition of Done:**

    Criteria that a user story needs to meet, before being marked as done.

33. **Definition of Ready:**

    Criteria that a user story needs to meet before going for development.

34. **DevOps:**

    A philosophy used in removing the silos between the development and operations of an IT organization.

35. **Digital Transformation:**

    The use and adoption of technology to transform businesses delivering products and services to their customers.

36. Design Thinking:

A human-centered approach to designing products, services, and processes to achieve maximum efficiency and less friction.

37. Encryption:

A process of encoding information and making it secure.

38. Epic:

A large work item, mainly a parent to multiple user stories.

39. Extreme Programming

An agile methodology for software development with a focus on programming best practices and includes pair programming.

40. Feature Bloat:

Including too many features in a product, without a logical reason or proven need.

41. Firewall:

A piece of hardware or a software application used to prevent unauthorized access to a computer or a network.

42. Full-Stack:

An engineer who works with both front-end and back-end technologies.

43. Function-as-a-Service:

It is a type of cloud computing technology made for developers to run, build, and deploy applications.

44. **General Availability:**

   A product that is available for the public to use.

45. **GOOB:**

   Get-out-of-the-building, meaning to go out and talk to the users.

46. **Go-to-Market:**

   Delivering your product or service to your customers by using all possible resources with a goal to maximize market share and earn revenue.

47. **Google Cloud Platform:**

   A cloud platform launched by Google.

48. **Hyper-competition:**

   Rapid competition in the market where the advantage is unsustainable.

49. **Hypervisor:**

   Software that runs a virtual machine application.

50. **IDE:**

   Integrated Development Environment, a bundle of software including code editors, compilers, and debuggers, etc.

51. **Infrastructure-as-a-Service:**

   An application of cloud technology, it provides computing resources, network, and storage to customers as a service.

52. **Intuitive Design:**

   Making products that are easy to use and a no-brainer.

53. **Landing Page:**

A one-pager website. Usually created for promotions and interest gathering.

54. **Market Validation:**

Identifying the need for your product in a market space.

55. **MEAN Stack:**

It is an open-source JavaScript framework, including MongoDB, Express, Angular, and Node.

56. **MERN Stack:**

It is an open-source JavaScript framework, including MongoDB, Express, React, and Node.

57. **Microsoft Azure:**

A cloud service provider launched by Microsoft to provide infrastructure on rent.

58. **Minimum Viable Product:**

The basic version of the product to attract early users.

59. **Monthly Recurring Revenue:**

The predictable monthly revenue for a business.

60. **MoSCoW Prioritization:**

It is a prioritization technique, classifying requirements as Must, Should, Could, and Would.

61. **Mockup:**

Design of a mobile app or website showing logic and structure of the system.

62. Name Server:

Connects a domain name with the IP address of the webserver and vice versa.

63. Network Security:

Policies and processes applied to secure a network from unauthorized access.

64. Objectives and Key Results:

A strategic tool for setting and tracking objectives.

65. Pair Programming:

An agile methodology for software development, where two programmers work on the same workstation together to deliver code.

66. Peer-to-Peer:

The connection between two computers, where both perform the required activities and there is no client-server relationship.

67. Planning Poker:

An agile work estimation technique mostly used in Scrum. It uses a deck of physical or digital cards and works on building consensus.

68. Platform-as-a-Service:

An application of cloud technology, it includes everything from IaaS, plus tools to build, test, and run your applications.

69. Podcast:

Digital audio files release over the internet as a form of episodic content.

70. **Product-Market Fit:**

It is the degree to which a product satisfies its intended market.

71. **Product Owner:**

A role in the scrum that works on creating and grooming the product backlog.

72. **Product Positioning:**

Promoting your product in a way that you control the way people perceive and feel about your product.

73. **Product Requirements Document:**

It is a document that lists down requirements of a product, its purpose, features, and behavior.

74. **Protocol:**

A set of rules for transmitting or sharing data between devices.

75. **Prototype:**

A sample or a model to test an idea or a proof of concept.

76. **Refactoring:**

Restructuring and improving code without changing the behavior or functionality.

77. **Release:**

The final version of the application launched after development or maintenance.

78. **Release Notes:**

Technical documentation released with the

product or an updated product, listing down features and fixes.

79. Retrospective:

    An event in the scrum where the team reflects on the previous sprint or time-box and evaluates its performance.

80. Stand up:

    Daily team meeting in Scrum.

81. Scope Creep:

    Uncontrolled changes in the scope are caused by customer feedback or internal team discussions. Usually increases the cost and complexity of the product.

82. Scrum Master:

    A role in the scrum that works as a servant leader and facilitates team activities. Replaces the traditional Project Manager in a Scrum team.

83. Software-as-a-Service:

    An application of cloud technology allowing access and use of the applications without installing them. The software and all the data reside somewhere on the cloud.

84. SWOT analysis:

    A strategic planning tool used to identify and document strengths, weaknesses, opportunities, and threats of a concept or a plan.

85. **Technical debt:**

    The cost of reworking or refactoring code when updating it for new features or bug fixes. This happens due to choosing easy or untidy solutions for a rushed release.

86. **Test-Driven Development:**

    An Agile methodology for software development, where unit tests are written first and then features are written to pass those unit tests.

87. **Traffic:**

    The total number of users coming to your website or application.

88. **Turnover Rate:**

    Percentage of customers who stopped using the product over a specified period.

89. **Use Case:**

    A scenario showing a certain feature of the product.

90. **User Flow:**

    A diagram showing the user's path or journey of interacting with the product for completing a task.

91. **User Persona:**

    The ideal profile of a fictional user. We used user personas for creating our marketing strategy and understanding the needs, pain points, and motivations of our users.

92. **User Story:**

    A single feature. A unit of requirement used in Scrum or other Agile methodologies.

93. **Usability testing:**

    Product testing with the aim of making it more usable and a no-brainer. This usually happens by working with the actual users and observing their interactions with the product.

94. **Unique selling proposition:**

    A feature or a benefit that makes the product unique and attractive to its targeted audience.

95. **Verification and Validation:**

    Testing a product for meeting the internal and industry-standard as well as customer expectations.

96. **Version Control:**

    Tools that help in keeping track of the changes in code or documentation.

97. **Velocity:**

    Speed of delivering features in each sprint or time box.

98. **Virtual Machine:**

    It represents a physical machine, but one physical machine can host several guests or virtual machines.

99. **Voice of Customer:**

    Finding data on customer needs and wants

by following a set of processes within an organization.

100. Waste:

A concept in Lean Software Development, meaning partially done work, bugs, extra features, and handoffs.

Conclusion

"
> "*People are more important than any process. Good people with a good process, will outperform good people with no process every time.*"
>
> *– Grady Booch, Software Architect and Co-inventor of Unified Modeling Language*

Getting an opportunity to work in Product Management can change your career trajectory and open lots of new and exciting avenues for you. You will learn new things, meet, and work with brilliant people, and have fun while creating incredible products for your customers. Finding the right mentor can also make things easier for you during and after this career pivot. They are like having a compass in uncharted waters; they won't tell you everything but will keep you pointed in the right direction.

I have been mentoring aspiring Product Managers for some time. While working with one of them, he mentioned my advice for getting him into the role appeared like a tried and tested process. At that time, it wasn't. I was just trying to build structure in an unstructured transition process so the people I work with don't lose their way. His comment made me realize this transition does require structure, and a step-by-step process, so I built one for all of you.

This book is a three-step process for you to prepare yourself to step into this role. The first step is getting to know this field better and understanding the pathways towards a career in Product Management. The second step is to find the right company and prepare yourself for the interview process. The third and final step is to guide you through all the important topics that are discussed and evaluated in a Product Management interview. This book has only one goal; once you reach its end, having worked through the action items, you will clear at least one Product Management interview and have a job offer to work as a Product Manager.

The knowledge here is coming from all the brilliant Product Managers and Technology leaders who have shared their work with the world and have given us fantastic products. They are the ones who have silently changed the world and our daily lives by bringing in more ease and comfort to everyone.

Product Managers are expected to show numerous traits, but the best and most useful of all is empathy. You will need much of it while solving problems for your customers and working with your teams, who have their own personalities, exposures, and biases. You need to show compassion but simultaneously apply your critical thinking skills to find a solution that works for everyone. Your job is to solve complex problems, and that's why it is crucial for a product's success.

A Product Manager is many things, but first and foremost, they are a leader, and with that, they are also a curious person with an enormous appetite for learning. Product Managers are resilient beings, and your decision to pivot your career in this direction has made me happy. I think you have chosen superbly.

I owe massive gratitude to everyone who helped me with this book, and I am especially grateful to my own mentors for being such generous teachers and facilitators. This book was my way of giving back and showing the way forward to the aspiring Product Managers out there. Learn, grow, and change the world!

I wish you all the best!

Irving Malcolm

Bibliography

1. *A/B Test*. (2020). ProductPlan. https://www.productplan.com/glossary/a-b-test/

2. *Fermi Problems*. (2019). Stem.org https://www.stem.org.uk/resources/collection/419670/fermi-problems

3. *How to price your product*. (2020). BDC. https://www.bdc.ca/en/articles-tools/marketing-sales-export/marketing/pricing-5-common-strategies

4. *Lean Software Development*. (2020). ProductPlan. https://www.productplan.com/glossary/lean-software-development/

5. Levitt, T. (1965). *Exploit the Product Life Cycle*. Harvard Business Review https://hbr.org/1965/11/exploit-the-product-life-cycle

6. *Manifesto for Agile Software Development*. (2001). Agile Manifesto. https://agilemanifesto.org/

7. Market Sizing – Estimating Product Potential (n.d.). Mindtools. https://www.mindtools.com/pages/article/market-sizing.html

8. *Principles behind the Agile Manifesto*. (2001). Agile Manifesto. https://agilemanifesto.org/principles.html

9. *Product Roadmap: Key Features, Types, Building Tips, and Roadmap Examples*. (2020). Altexsoft.

https://www.altexsoft.com/blog/business/product-roadmap-key-features-common-types-and-roadmap-building-tips/

10. Taylor, J. (2020) *Business metrics vs. KPIs.* Klipfolio. https://www.klipfolio.com/blog/business-metrics-vs-kpis

11. *Tech economics: scale and scope.* (2019). ParkerSoftware. https://www.parkersoftware.com/blog/tech-economics-scale-and-scope/

12. *The SAR Method for Product Management Interview Questions.* (2020). Product School. https://productschool.com/blog/product-management-2/the-sar-method-for-product-management-interview-questions/

13. *Think Like a Product Manager.* (2017). YouTube. https://www.youtube.com/watch?v=omjWcMNgWMY

14. *What are vanity metrics?* (n.d.). Tableau. https://www.tableau.com/learn/articles/vanity-metrics

15. *What is an Algorithm.* Think Automation. (2020). https://www.thinkautomation.com/eli5/what-is-an-algorithm-an-in-a-nutshell-explanation/

16. *What is DevOps.* (2021). Amazon Web Services. https://aws.amazon.com/devops/what-is-devops/

17. *What is Kanban.* (2019). Atlassian. https://www.atlassian.com/agile/kanban

18. *What is Scrum.* (n.d.). Scrum.org https://www.scrum.org/resources/what-is-scrum

19. *What Product Metrics Matter?* (2021). ProductPlan. https://www.productplan.com/learn/product-metrics-matter/

Recommended Reading

1. Ariely, D. (2010). Predictably Irrational, Revised and Expanded Edition: The Hidden Forces That Shape Our Decisions (Revised and Expanded ed.). Harper Perennial.

2. Aronson, E., & Aronson, J. (2018). The Social Animal Twelfth Edition (Twelfth ed.). Worth Publishers.

3. Banfield, R., Eriksson, M., & Walkingshaw, N. (2017). Product Leadership: How Top Product Managers Launch Awesome Products and Build Successful Teams (1st ed.). O'Reilly Media.

4. Berger, J. (2016). Contagious: Why Things Catch On (1st ed.). Simon & Schuster.

5. Brafman, O. (2021). Sway: The Irresistible Pull of Irrational Behavior (Unabridged ed.). Highbridge Audio and Blackstone Publishing.

6. Brown, B. (2018). Dare to Lead: Brave Work. Tough Conversations. Whole Hearts. (First Edition). Random House.

7. Cagan, M. (2017). Inspired: How to Create Tech Products Customers Love (Silicon Valley Product Group) (2nd ed.). Wiley.

8. Cagan, M., & Jones, C. (2020). Empowered: Ordinary People, Extraordinary Products (Silicon Valley Product Group) (1st ed.). Wiley.

9. Chabris, C., & Simons, D. (2011). The Invisible Gorilla: How Our Intuitions Deceive Us (Reprint ed.). Harmony.

10. Christensen, C. M. (2016). The Innovator's Dilemma: When New Technologies Cause Great Firms to Fail (Management of Innovation and Change) (Illustrated ed.). Harvard Business Review Press.

11. Christensen, C. M., Dillon, K., Hall, T., & Duncan, D. S. (2016). Competing Against Luck: The Story of Innovation and Customer Choice (1st ed.). Harper Business.

12. Cialdini, R. B. (2006). Influence: The Psychology of Persuasion, Revised Edition (Revised ed.). Harper Business.

13. Collins, J., & Porras, J. (2002). Built to Last: Successful Habits of Visionary Companies (Harper Business Essentials) (3rd ed.). Collins Business.

14. Csikszentmihalyi, M. (2008). Flow: The Psychology of Optimal Experience (Harper Perennial Modern Classics) (1st ed.). Harper Perennial Modern Classics.

15. Diamandis, P. H., & Kotler, S. (2020). The Future Is Faster Than You Think: How Converging Technologies Are Transforming Business, Industries, and Our Lives (Exponential Technology Series). Simon & Schuster.

16. Doerr, J., & Page, L. (2018). Measure What Matters: How Google, Bono, and the Gates Foundation Rock the World with OKRs (Illustrated ed.). Portfolio.

17. Duckworth, A. (2018). Grit: The Power of Passion and Perseverance (Illustrated ed.). Scribner.

18. Eyal, N., & Hoover, R. (2014). Hooked: How to Build Habit-Forming Products (Illustrated ed.). Portfolio.

19. Fishkin, R. (2018). Lost and Founder: A Painfully Honest Field Guide to the Startup World (Illustrated ed.). Portfolio.

20. Fried, J., & Hansson, H. D. (2010a). Rework (1st ed.). Currency.

21. Fried, J., & Hansson, H. D. (2010b). Rework (1st ed.). Currency.

22. Gladwell, M. (2002). The Tipping Point: How Little Things Can Make a Big Difference. Back Bay Books.

23. Godin, S. (2007). Purple Cow: Transform Your Business by Being Remarkable (1st Edition). Penguin Books.

24. Grove, A. S. (1999). Only the Paranoid Survive: How to Exploit the Crisis Points That Challenge Every Company (1st Edition). Currency.

25. Hastings, R., & Meyer, E. (2020). No Rules Rules: Netflix and the Culture of Reinvention (Illustrated ed.). Penguin Press.

26. 26. Heath, C., & Heath, D. (2007). Made to Stick: Why Some Ideas Survive and Others Die (1st ed.). Random House.

27. Horowitz, B. (2014). The Hard Thing About Hard Things: Building a Business When There Are No Easy Answers. Harper Business.

28. Iyengar, S. (2011). The Art of Choosing (Illustrated ed.). Twelve.

29. Kahneman, D. (2013). Thinking, Fast and Slow (1st ed.). Farrar, Straus and Giroux.

30. Kleon, A. (2012). Steal Like an Artist: 10 Things Nobody Told You About Being Creative (1st ed.). Workman Publishing.

31. Knapp, J. (2016). Sprint: How to Solve Big Problems and Test New Ideas in Just Five Days (1st ed.). Simon & Schuster.

32. Lencioni, P. (2002). The Five Dysfunctions of a Team: A Leadership Fable (1st ed.). Jossey-Bass.

33. Luca, M., & Bazerman, M. H. (2020). The Power of Experiments: Decision Making in a Data-Driven World (The MIT Press) (Illustrated ed.). The MIT Press.

34. MacLeod, H. (2009). Ignore Everybody: and 39 Other Keys to Creativity (First Edition). Portfolio.

35. Martinez, G. A. (2018). Chaos Monkeys: Obscene Fortune and Random Failure in Silicon Valley (Reprint ed.). Harper Paperbacks.

36. Mehta, N., Agashe, A., & Detroja, P. (2017). Swipe to Unlock: The Primer on Technology and Business Strategy. CreateSpace Independent Publishing Platform.

37. Norman, D. (2013). The Design of Everyday Things: Revised and Expanded Edition (Revised ed.). Basic Books.

38. Odell, J. (2020). How to Do Nothing: Resisting the Attention Economy. Melville House.

39. Patton, J., & Economy, P. (2014). User Story Mapping: Discover the Whole Story, Build the Right Product (1st ed.). O'Reilly Media.

40. Ries, E. (2011). The Lean Startup: How Today's Entrepreneurs Use Continuous Innovation to Create Radically Successful Businesses (Illustrated ed.). Currency.

41. Rosenzweig, P. (2014). The Halo Effect: . . . and the Eight Other Business Delusions That Deceive Managers (Reissue ed.). Free Press.

42. Ross, A. (2017). The Industries of the Future (Reprint ed.). Simon & Schuster.

43. Schmidt, E., & Rosenberg, J. (2017). How Google Works (Reprint ed.). Grand Central Publishing.

44. Scott, K. (2019). Radical Candor (Be a Kick-Ass Boss Without Losing Your Humanity (Revised, Updated)) (1st ed.). St. Martin's Press.

45. Sinek, S. (2011). Start with Why: How Great Leaders Inspire Everyone to Take Action (Illustrated ed.). Portfolio.

46. Singer, R. (2020). Shape Up: Stop Running in Circles and Ship Work that Matters. Basecamp.

47. Stone, B. (2017). The Upstarts: How Uber, Airbnb, and the Killer Companies of the New Silicon Valley Are Changing the World (Large type / Large print ed.). Little, Brown and Company.

48. Thiel, P., & Masters, B. (2014). Zero to One: Notes on Startups, or How to Build the Future (Illustrated ed.). Currency.

49. Vance, A. (2017). Elon Musk: Tesla, SpaceX, and the Quest for a Fantastic Future (Illustrated ed.). Ecco.

50. Voss, C., & Raz, T. (2018). Never Split the Difference: Negotiating As If Your Life Depended On It. Harper Business.

About the Author

Irving Malcolm lives in London, where he runs a Management consultancy firm.

Having started out as a project manager before pivoting into Product Management, he has a wealth of knowledge and experience he is passionate about sharing with aspiring and new Product Managers. His favourite way to help others make that transition into a successful Product Manager career is through writing books.